Dedication

For our next generation…

Kade, Brody, Joel, Shepard, Abbie, Claire, Amelia,
Ava Grace, Hannah, Caleb, Norah, June, Max

Raising Kids for Tomorrow's World:
12 Keys to Preserving the Faith

Stan and Cheryl Schuermann

Published by Pen It! Publications, LLC in the U.S.A.
812-371-4128 www.penitpublications.com

ISBN: 978-1-63984-124-0
Edited by Dina Husseini

Unless otherwise indicated, Scripture quotations are taken from The Holy Bible: English Standard Version, copyright 2001 by Crossway Bibles, a publishing ministry of Good News Publishers.

Paul's Ministry to the Thessalonians
1 Thessalonians 2:1-14

For you yourselves know, brothers, that our coming to you was not in vain. But though we had already suffered and been shamefully treated at Philippi, as you know, we had boldness in our God to declare to you the gospel of God in the midst of much conflict. For our appeal does not spring from error or impurity or any attempt to deceive, but just as we have been approved by God to be entrusted with the gospel, so we speak, not to please man, but to please God who tests our hearts.

For we never came with words of flattery, as you know, nor with a pretext for greed—God is witness. Nor did we seek glory from people, whether from you or from others, though we could have made demands as apostles of Christ. But we were gentle among you, like a nursing mother taking care of her own children. So, being affectionately desirous of you, we were ready to share with you not only the gospel of God but also our own selves, because you had become very dear to us.

For you remember, brothers, our labor and toil: we worked night and day, that we might not be a burden to any of you, while we proclaimed to you the gospel of God. You are witnesses, and God also, how holy and righteous and blameless was our conduct toward you believers. For you know how, like a father with his children, we exhorted each one of you and encouraged you and charged you to walk in a manner worthy of God, who calls you into his own kingdom and glory.

And we also thank God constantly for this, that when you received the word of God, which you heard from us, you accepted it not as the word of men but as what it really is, the word of God, which is at work in you believers. For you, brothers, became imitators of the churches of God in Christ Jesus that are in Judea. For you suffered the same things from your own countrymen as they did from the Jews.

Table of Contents

Introduction

Becoming a Parent

When I (Stan) was a twenty-four-year-old graduate student, a nurse placed an eight-pound baby boy into my arms. Not even sure of the proper way to hold him, I looked at this baby and then at my beautiful and exhausted wife.

She smiled. "You're a father now; you have a son. What do you think?"

Think? Surely, I wanted to be a good father and protect my son. I imagined the fun we would have and wondered all those things parents wonder.

What will he be like? Will I be a good dad?

The desire was there, no doubt. Even with the good examples we had in our own parents, what Cheryl and I did *not* know about parenting was *a lot*. We believed a child is a gift from the hand of God. And, in receiving our new son, we had been called to this grand adventure of parenting.

Not only did I hold new life in my arms, but I also had new life in me. Christ was introduced to me as a young child and more fully revealed to me during college. There, I became a Christian and began to study the Bible.

Our new son, David, entered into a covenant relationship with God through our family. God had

1

much to teach us about believing him. As David grew, so did we. In a few short years, God added three more sons to our home, Matthew, Andrew and Daniel.

As they grew, so did we.

While we could not see even one minute into the future, we knew our young boys would follow someone in their effort to find happiness. If they did not know God, it would be natural for them to follow the crowd or someone in the crowd, or even declare like Pharaoh, "Who is the Lord that I should obey his voice…I do not know the Lord…" (Exodus 5:2).

Fortunately, we saw our goal as parents was not merely to conform our sons to a standard, but to joyfully introduce them to God. Our task was to teach them of the one who created them, loves them, and plans for their flourishing.

Thus, our opportunity as parents through our words and life is to paint a portrait of the One our children do not yet know. With broad, sweeping brushstrokes and the finest detail, we create a beautiful portrait of the unseen God. Through our illustrating, our children will come to understand he is the Lord and desire to obey his voice. Whom your children follow will be the most important ongoing decision of their lives.

When you receive a child into your covenant family, by birth or through adoption, the "long view" will give perspective on the joys as well as the daily trials that are sure to come. Each day presents opportunities to illustrate something beautiful about Christ.

Becoming a Pastor to Our Children

Several years ago, I prepared to teach through Paul's letters to the church in Thessalonica. In reading I Thessalonians 2, I studied Paul's description of his ministry. He used terms "like a mother" and "like a father." Though he had no children of his own, Paul obviously considered himself to be like a parent as he pastored his young church.

That was interesting enough and worth exploring further, but then I came to verse 13. Paul wrote, "And we also thank God constantly for this, that when you received the word of God, which you heard from us, you accepted it not as the word of men but as what it really is, the word of God, which is at work in you believers" (I Thessalonians 2:13).

That's it!

Paul gives thanks for exactly what we desire for our own children. Doesn't every Christian parent desire their children would, like the Thessalonians, receive the word of God which they hear from us?

And not only receive it, but value it because they understand it is not just our word, but the Word of God? Our praise would undoubtedly echo Paul's as we see how God has become the authority in our child's life instead of the culture...or their emotions...or friends.

This section of text came to life for me. I knew there must be more for parents here and eagerly pursued these verses. In verse 1, Paul wrote, "...our coming to you was not in vain." If verse 13 is what we hope and labor for most, then verse 1 is what we fear most; all of our years of labor, teaching, and instruction and all the giving of ourselves for our children's sakes would be in vain. We have heard expressions of concern from parents who tell us their child wandered from the faith. Even Paul experienced this in other locations.

I Thessalonians Chapter 2 is a wonderful gift given to parents. We could not have received more from Paul if we had interviewed him in person in our living room. Paul recounts for the Thessalonians, and for us, exactly what he did--as if we have been handed the keys to Paul's pastoring and parenting in his young churches.

Twelve keys (or passages) emerge from verses 1-14. The word 'passages' can be used to indicate the course by which a person passes or travels to get to a destination. Christian parents have a clear destination...to lead their children to love God, believe and embrace his Son, and understand and obey his Word. Parenting is a journey for both parents and children!

Each of the twelve Passages are illustrated with three short chapters and are helpful for parents, grandparents, aunts, uncles, and anyone who is a loving mentor to children and teens. Through the pages of *Raising Kids for Tomorrow's World,* theological truth is presented in a practical way. We, the authors, desire that readers will understand the theology and engage it, allow the wisdom of God's Word to inform their parenting practice, and be encouraged to live by faith. What we do today in our homes will impact our children's spiritual walk tomorrow.

Parents, it is never too late to start parenting well. If you are reading this and your children are well on their way, some even in directions taking them far from the protection of God, we invite you to engage this resource.

To those whose hearts are breaking for their teens and adult children, you may draw encouragement from Charles Spurgeon. "But Jesus still commands, 'Bring him to me.'" Spurgeon then encourages us, "Never must we cease to pray until they cease to breathe. No case is hopeless while Jesus lives."[1]

You were born for this time and the time to come. So were your children.

Stan

Passage I

Discover Boldness

"...we had boldness in our God to declare to you
the gospel of God..."
-- I Thessalonians 2:2

Everyone has a theological framework, or worldview, influencing everything they do, including how they parent their children.

The Apostle Paul's increasing knowledge of God gave him great confidence and boldness to preach the gospel.

Paul understood the power of the gospel to bring about God's purposes in gathering a people for himself.

Chapter 1

Everyone is a Theologian

Imagine you are planning to build a grand timber framed home. (If you are reading this in July, imagine Montana. If you are reading this in January, imagine Hawaii.) Your desire is to provide secure shelter for you and your family and anyone you invite inside—a safe place to live and grow.

If you choose the right source, everything you need for building the structure of your home is *delivered* to you in a kit on a giant semi-trailer. When you are ready to begin the assembly process, you have options. You can start constructing according to the design or go freelance and assemble according to your own creative impulses.

Either way, you begin with the kit you *received.*

From the first timber you tackle, you realize the first truth: how the pieces fit together matters. The only way to ensure the structure you build will be sound is to carefully connect the pieces according to the design.

Some of the sturdiest timbers will provide the foundation for the entire structure. Others are designed to fit into these foundation timbers and be supported by them. If the structure is not fitted together as designed, the building will lack strength to withstand the power of the storms that are sure to rage against it.

R.C. Sproul is famous for saying, "Everyone's a theologian."[1] This is even the title of one of his books. By this, he means everyone has a set of beliefs about God. Even those who operate as if there is no God still have a theology. For the Christian, our theology is delivered to us from the truth revealed in Scripture. As we gain more wisdom, our understanding increases. You could say our theology is assembled by carefully considering what we have received. There is never a need to create our own theology.

Although most of our children will not build their own home, all of our children are in the process of assembling their theology, their operating system or worldview. If we (and our children) are assembling a sound theological framework, we will have four foundational timbers supporting the entire structure. Any coherent worldview must provide satisfactory answers to these questions:

1. **Origin**—How did we get here? Is there a God? What is he like?
2. **Meaning**—What does this life mean? What is our purpose for existing? How do we understand evil and suffering?
3. **Morality**—How do we know what is right and what is wrong? What is the basis for ethics and morality?

4. **Destiny**—What happens when we die? Where is history headed?

When we consider these four foundational timbers, there is no doubt why the question of origin is first. From our answer to: "How did we get here?" will flow the understanding necessary to address all the others.

It also follows that if we have no good answer to this question, we will have unconnected answers to the rest. In our attempt to find meaning in life, the only tools left in our toolbox would be our own speculations and musings.

What if your children have not assembled the pieces by the time they are in high school? Or when they leave for college? They may be tempted to adjust their theological pieces to accommodate the "theology" of their friends and the influential people around them. This is why, as a parent or as a grandparent, you have a most important role in leading your children to discover, fall in love with, and embrace the truths God has revealed.

A.W. Tozer, an American Christian pastor and author, said, "What comes into our minds when we think about God is the most important thing about us."[2]

Our task as parents is to present to our children a truthful and coherent understanding of God and life.

Consider and Apply:

1. Examine your beliefs about origin, meaning, morality, and destiny. Do your core beliefs come from a biblical framework, or are they collected from various belief systems and possibly your own interpretation of reality?

2. "Worldviews are caught more than taught. Like a cold, most people 'catch' their worldview beliefs from the culture around them. If we never stop and examine our worldview, we will still have one, but it may not be the right one"[3] (Stonestreet and Kunkle). Where are *your* children catching their worldview?

Resources:

- John Stonestreet and Brett Kunkle, *A Practical Guide to Culture: Helping the Next Generation Navigate Today's World* (David C. Cook, 2017)
- Albert Mohler provides a daily analysis of current events from a Christian worldview called *The Daily Briefing.*
  See albertmohler.com /the-briefing.

Chapter 2

From Calling to Boldness

At the beginning of I Thessalonians Chapter 2, Paul states he had boldness. Boldness is a grand idea; although, as parents consider the challenges of raising children for tomorrow's world, the idea of boldness may seem elusive.

Do we really need boldness and confidence? Could we just settle for apprehension?

We already have apprehension working really well. But Paul uses the word *boldness*, and boldness even in the midst of conflict.

If we desire boldness in raising children, we should follow the Apostle Paul's example. Paul was not bold in his own abilities. He states he had boldness in God. In his commentary on I Thessalonians 2:2, John Calvin writes, "In the meantime he [Paul] stood firm and undaunted, from which it appears that he was held up by the hand of God; for this is what he means when he says that he was emboldened."[1] Paul's boldness came from faith rightly placed.

Mankind's story is full of bold leaders, and all had a sense they were the person at that moment to change individual lives and the course of history. They believed they had a destiny to fulfill as part of a grand story bigger than themselves. This is true of both virtuous leaders and despots. Their lives were given to a purpose, and they had a mission to complete.

Paul understood he was part of God's eternal story—the story of how God is pursuing and calling out and redeeming a people for himself. In Galatians 1:15-16, Paul mentions he was set apart for this gospel ministry to the Gentiles even before his birth. Until his dramatic conversion to Christ, Paul could not have been more removed from the Gentiles.

He was raised as an orthodox Jew who kept himself separate from the Gentile world. He was a Pharisee, zealous for Judaism and he opposed every form of religion that threatened it. For a time, he even became a violent persecutor of the new sect of Christ followers (Acts 22:3-4, 26:9-11).

After his conversion, Paul began proclaiming Christ to his fellow Jews, but his ministry would eventually lead him to the Gentiles. To accomplish his mission, he traveled throughout the Roman empire from about A.D. 38 until his death in Rome around A.D. 64.

On one journey, Paul, Silvanus (Silas) and Timothy arrived in Thessalonica where they proclaimed the gospel message and began a ministry. A small fellowship of believers was born so Paul and his fellow ministers stayed for several months teaching and strengthening the believers in the doctrines of their new faith.

They eventually left Thessalonica and continued on their ministry to other regions, but like any parent, Paul was concerned about how the young Thessalonian church was faring. He wrote a letter (the letter we now study) and sent Timothy back to check on them. Parents everywhere can certainly understand this sense of concern.

Paul wrote this letter during the time he was ministering in Corinth. While there, Paul encountered such opposition that the Lord appeared to encourage him. Luke records this for us in Acts 18:9-11. "And the Lord said to Paul one night in a vision, 'Do not be afraid, but go on speaking and do not be silent, for I am with you...for I have many in this city who are my people.'"

Paul was strengthened and understood he was to continue speaking and ministering. He was comforted knowing the Lord would be with him while he tended to the needs of the people. "As if he [God] should have said, I will help you, that you may not fail my people whose minister I have appointed you to be"[2] (Calvin).

Paul had a job to complete and people to complete. Confidence and boldness come as we have success and see God at work in our children and in ourselves.

Consider and Apply:

1. Boldness comes from confidence and propels you forward against all odds. How does understanding the narrative of God's world, from Adam to Jesus Christ, from creation through redemption to future glory, give you confidence and boldness in raising your children?
2. Read I Thessalonians 5:24, Hebrews 10:35-36, Psalm 103:17-18. How do these verses encourage you in your parenting journey?
3. When does your confidence as a parent break down? Though we may be weary, though we may not know what to do, God calls us to keep working and look to the promised fruit.

Chapter 3

The Gospel

A Television Story

Do you ever feel like you shower your children with love and incredibly wise counsel—only to have them reject your instruction and go their own way? Several years ago, we saw a thirty second commercial depicting a father, his child, and her desire for freedom.

The scene opens with a father giving instruction to his young daughter sitting in the driver's seat of a car. She listens for a time but soon grows tired of his instructions. She is ready to be free, to be on her own, and make her own choices.

The father offers her the keys to this privilege. The girl eagerly grabs the keys and is transformed into a young woman. As she drives away, the word LOVE is displayed on the screen, and we hear the father saying, "This is why we bought a [brand of car]."

Everything we observe him doing is out of love for her.

As the commercial ends, we hope this young woman will enjoy the freedom granted to her. We also hope this father's love and care will be rewarded and his daughter protected by her careful obedience to her father's loving advice.

At the same time, we fear what will happen if she rejects his instruction. What if we rewrote the ending of this hypothetical story according to the history of mankind?

In her new story, like ours, she listens to others and believes her father's advice is too restrictive. She sees his rules as barriers to her self-directed freedom rather than as guides which will lead her on a path to true freedom and happiness.

She listens to the false counsel of others, those who do not love her, and decides to leave the protection of obedience. Although all she wanted was to be free, her experiment ends in catastrophe.

What would any father do? He goes after her. Motivated by love for his daughter, he enters her world to do whatever is necessary to affect her rescue. She is now a law breaker, and a ransom must be paid for her to go free.

Here is the good news!

Having resources to pay the needed ransom, the father joyfully and fully pays the debt. With all accounts settled, he gathers her up and brings her home to enjoy their relationship, fully restored.

Now here is the recorded history with real people and real consequences.

Our Story

The story of mankind began with the first two members of the human race, Adam and Eve. Just like the father in the car commercial, God instructed them, inviting them to enjoy every good and choice thing which had been created (See Genesis 2:15-16).

In their instruction to children, most parents will include both an invitation and a warning. Enjoy all of this...avoid that. In the Garden of Eden, God listed only one prohibition, one danger to avoid.

Sounds easy, right? What could go wrong?

Unfortunately, the danger did not appear to Adam and Eve to be dangerous at all. To them, the "danger" appeared attractive, even desirable. And their disposition, like ours, was to follow their desires. This is the same desire for self-rule we see in our two-year-old and hear in our teen and in ourselves. We want what we want when *we* want it.

Adam and Eve rejected the wisdom and protection of God and took their own counsel. They decided to get for themselves what they wanted, thinking their independence (freedom) would open the doors wide for them to find happiness. Through their disobedience, Adam and Eve lost the inheritance reserved for them and established the course all mankind would eventually follow.

Their predicament is now our predicament. Our need is great—not merely for good advice or a good example to follow, but to be forgiven and restored. We also must be made new, with a new mind that desires what our Creator wants for us.

How will God restore blessing to us, his banished ones?

We need a substitute, one who will pay the penalty for our crimes. And one who will grant us a new status and provide the holy standing necessary to be children of the eternal God. The substitute is God himself, who came after us in the person of his Son.

Jesus Christ lived the perfect sinless life that no other human can live. As a sinless man, he offered himself and exchanged his life for the helpless sinner. This is the gospel Paul speaks of in I Thessalonians 2. In offering us his Son, God made a way for us to know and be welcomed by him.

Our human story began with our Father's love for his children and his invitation to enjoy all he has provided for us. It is also the story of our rebellion. But our story does not end there for the Father came on a rescue mission to restore us so we might enjoy even greater blessings and a new future. The benefits have already been won for us and we receive them simply by believing.

This is the good news of the gospel.

Consider and Apply:

1. Read John 1:1-13. Note verse 12. Have you believed this great news of the gospel? In believing, do you understand you are welcomed to God as your father? Describe the privileges of being reconciled to God.
2. Consider this quote by John Piper. "God is most glorified in you when you are most satisfied in Him."[1] How does this quote relate to your life and to your role as a parent?

Passage II

Persevere in the Midst of Conflict

"...in the midst of much conflict."

-- I Thessalonians 2:2

Just as the apostles experienced resistance to Christ and his gospel in the training up of the churches, parents are often hindered in the training up of their own children.

This is why parenting regularly occurs "in the midst of much conflict."

Not only does this conflict come from forces outside our families but we also observe a state of conflict residing inside of us and our children.

Regardless of the challenges we may face, our mission as parents remains the same—to impart the knowledge and love of God to our children.

Chapter 4

Caught in the Devil's Bargain

Sitting around a campfire with friends many years ago, we took part in a game called "Two Truths and a Lie." In this game, each person made three statements and everyone else tried to figure out which one was the lie. It was just a game, an icebreaker. In our real world, mankind has an adversary who uses lies to produce terrible consequences.

There was a time in history when there were no lies. God created mankind in his image, perfect in soul and body. His image *did* shine in Adam and Eve, for after their creation, God declared everything was "very good" (Genesis 1:31). They lived in joyful obedience to God's commandments in the Garden created especially for them. Our adversary had a plan to change that.

Joni Mitchell seemed to accurately recall this history when, in her song "Woodstock," she acknowledged, "We've got to get ourselves back to the garden." [1] Though created in God's image, we are not who we should be.

Nor are we free!

This is why we are always trying to get back to the garden in our search for that elusive freedom.

What makes Mitchell's lyrics so insightful is she goes on to correctly diagnose our condition. The song continues by declaring humans are caught in the devil's bargain. Sadly, this is true; the Bible says we lost our freedom when we were ensnared by the devil's trickery.

God gave instructions to Adam to enjoy everything in the Garden of Eden freely—everything except for one tree, the tree of the Knowledge of Good and Evil. In Genesis 2:8-3:7, Moses records what happened there when Adam and Eve fell from their privileged position. Satan, whom Scripture calls "the father of lies" (John 8:44), was intent on destroying God's image bearers and ruining the human race. As he engaged Eve in conversation, his first goal was to weaken her confidence in God's instruction and his character. By doing so, she could eventually be led to disregard God's commands and choose according to her own desires. His game plan is easy to see: "One Question and Two Lies."

One Question: *"Did God actually say?"* (Genesis 3:1) Satan created confusion in Eve's mind, as if he had said, "Are you sure?" With this question, Satan sowed sufficient doubt to allow him to proceed.

Lie #1: *"You will not surely die!"* (Genesis 3:4) With this bold lie, Satan blatantly contradicted God's command. Now lacking confidence in God's words, Eve believed the lie. As a result, her fear of the promised consequence was removed.

Lie #2: *"You will be like God!"* (Genesis 3:5) Satan openly accused God of falsehood. He appealed to Eve's basic desire to throw off the yoke and become an independent creature. What could be better than to be like God and determine for herself what was good and what was evil?

Adam and Eve left the protection of God's Word to follow their senses and desires. From Satan's perspective, his evil game worked perfectly. Sadly, this is not just our ancient history. Satan's plan for our children *and* for us is still the same.

One Question and Two Lies is played out daily, often leading to disaster. Sin's diagram is not complicated. As with Eve, it always starts with wrong thinking. John Calvin said, "Satan dazzles us with an appearance of what is right."[2]

Thus, we are drawn in.

God's Word is given to help us understand what our hearts long for and to guide us to the happiness we seek. We were designed for this *dependent* life which provides us with great protection. The problem is, since we first fell for Satan's lie that God is withholding good from us, our chief bent is to be *independent.*

We believe the best chance we have at happiness is to make up our own minds about what is right and wrong. We may call it "freedom," but that is just the word we use when we want what is outside the protection of obedience.

In the beginning, the faith Adam and Eve had in the character of God was the best guardian of their hearts and of all their senses. They were caught in a trap, the devil's bargain. Our task as Christian parents is to steep ourselves in God's truth and teach our children about the character of God. This is the only way to stand strong against Satan's game of deceit. Though Satan has a plan for our destruction, God has a plan for our deliverance.

Consider and Apply:

1. What are some traps you and your children face on a daily basis?

2. A common goal of parenting is to teach independence. How do we teach our children to be independent in the world yet dependent on God?

3. How will you help your children discern these two great competing theologies concerning happiness? (1) Happiness is assured by obedience to God. (2) Happiness is assured by obedience to my desires.

4. We are directed in life by the way we think about things. Wrong thinking often launches wrong-doing. A critical goal of parenting is to help our children *recognize* wrong thinking and understand its sources. This is the great challenge, especially to parents of preteens and teens. The consequences only become greater with age because they involve relationships and attachments.

Chapter 5

Raising Little Pharaoh

In Exodus 5:2, Pharaoh said to Moses, "Who is the Lord that I should obey his voice and let Israel go? I do not know the Lord..." Translation: "Who is the Lord as compared to me? I am king here!" It is reasonable that Pharaoh should ask such a question. He believed he was the big king, and he was naturally unwilling to obey another.

Moses began to teach Pharaoh important lessons about the Lord, the true King of Kings. God supplied Moses with an arsenal of powerful illustrations, including an assortment of plagues. Even with frogs, flies, and diseases descending upon his people, Pharaoh did not learn and did not submit to the true King (Exodus 14). As a result, his entire army of chariots and horsemen drowned in the sea.

Though our children may not voice the same question as Pharaoh, their young minds ask "Who are *you*, Mom/Dad, that I should obey you? I want to be king!" As Tom Petty sang, "It's good to be king and have your own way."[1] This is the challenge to any authority, and this is the biggest challenge of parenting.

Parenting is an effort to conform the wills of little people who want to be independent, who do not want their wills to be conformed to you or any other authority. Our children have this part of their theology well established. The basic nature we all have, from the first human, Adam, to our newborns, results in every one of us wanting to be king. This is why a parent's instruction of the important wisdom necessary for life meets with such resistance.

Like Moses, we have an opportunity to teach our children who we are and why we should be obeyed. At the same time, we point them to who God is and why he should be obeyed. We do this by demonstrating the constancy of our love for them, the blessings of obedience, as well as the consequences of not obeying. In addition, we model our love for God and our own desire to obey.

A great place to begin is by memorizing Ephesians 6:1-4 as a family. "Children, obey your parents in the Lord, for this is right. 'Honor your father and mother' (this is the first commandment with a promise), 'that it may go well with you and that you may live long in the land.' Fathers, do not provoke your children to anger, but bring them up in the discipline and instruction of the Lord."

What do we want our children to understand?

1. *Obeying God is a family effort.* God wants the very best for all of us. Obedience is not just for the children! Refer often to God's instructions in the Bible and the call for all to obey them.
2. *Obedience brings blessing.* God says obedience is the right thing to do. It comes with a promise that it will result in good things. Talk with your children about what "well" could mean in the verse. Our instruction should be seen as essential guides to their safety and happiness rather than onerous prohibitions. In this way, they will come to love God's law and to love wisdom.
3. *Obedience shows love to parents and to God.* Our obedience demonstrates that we love and believe our Heavenly Father. When children obey their parents, they honor not only them but also God.

Our hearts will be inclined toward instruction when we know the character and intent of the one instructing us. As our children grow older, our task is to move them from, "Who is the Lord?" to "I know the Lord and I want to obey Him!"

Consider and Apply:

1. John Stott said, "Wise parents recognize that not all the non-conforming responses of childhood deserve to be styled rebellion…It is by experiment that children discover the limits of their liberty and the quality of their parent's love."[2] How do you determine if your child's negative behavior is rebellion or merely immaturity?

2. Since our children have a nature that wants to be king, they want *what* they want and usually *when* they want it. However, they often lack the discernment to recognize what is true and what is the counterfeit. How do we begin to create in them a desire for true things that will ultimately satisfy?

3. Psalms and Proverbs are full of praise for the protection we receive by loving God's testimonies. Read Psalm 119:9,16, 24 and Proverbs 4:4-6.

Chapter 6

Our Mission Remains the Same

If you are over the age of three, you will remember the year 2020. It is true no generation has escaped the dread of some catastrophic threat to the world. We watch the streaming news as the world we *know* rapidly becomes the world we *knew*. When bad news is only followed by worse news, we can also experience a loss of hope and a sense of dread. We often cannot control the time and circumstance of our lives.

In *The Fellowship of the Ring* (The Lord of the Rings #1), J.R.R. Tolkien's characters said it well:

"I wish it need not have happened in my time," said Frodo.

"So, do I," said Gandalf, "and so do all who live to see such times. But that is not for them to decide. All we have to decide is what to do with the time that is given us."[1]

Every one of us will encounter trials. How do we stay focused on our mission of raising our children well—even in the midst of conflict?

In April 2019, we traveled to France for two weeks. For three days, we absorbed the sights and images of the battles and struggles that took place in Normandy seventy-five years prior. A highlight was exploring the town of Sainte Mere-Église near Utah Beach. This ancient town was one of the first to be liberated by the Americans. It was first in the grand allied mission to liberate all of France and finally, even more grand, to liberate all of Europe.

The surrounding fields and the town itself became the scene of fierce fighting as the paratroopers of the 82nd and 101st Airborne Divisions battled through the night and into the morning of June 6, 1944. Every soldier's struggle was epic, something most had never faced before.

These battles were fought mainly by young men, some as young as eighteen. Even with all of the tactical planning, for most of the troops, everything at the beginning of this grand liberation campaign went wrong. At nearly every turn, it seemed as if the mission would end in catastrophe.

At the Airborne Museum in Sainte Mere-Église, we listened to the recorded voices of the fighters recalling their stories. No matter where they landed and no matter what they encountered, their *first* goal was to get oriented, to figure out where they were.

During the jumps, most landed far from their target. They and their fellow soldiers and the needed equipment were scattered everywhere. For every soldier, their *next* need was to gather their resources, find fellow soldiers, form up, and determine, "Who is with us?" After they understood who was with them and what equipment they had, the soldiers *finally* began to move out to complete their assigned mission.

We noted the soldiers' mission was exactly the same as before they encountered the hardships. According to their stories, they persevered in order to complete their mission. In a similar way, Luke records for us in Acts 20:17-24 how Paul gathered together the elders of the church in Ephesus. He reminded them of how he had preached and ministered in every place. He knew he would face new hardships and assured his people that his mission would remain the same.

All parents face hardship, whether challenges with children, marriage, jobs, or even a worldwide pandemic.

Ask yourself, *has our mission changed as a result of hardship and conflict? Has Satan driven us off course?*

Some challenges are, indeed, epic and cause tremendous loss. Some are simply annoyances. In the midst of any battle…get your bearings, gather your resources, and persevere. Remember, perseverance is not the goal. It was not the goal for those young soldiers in France.

They would all tell you they persevered *in order to* complete their mission.

Consider and Apply:

1. If asked to describe your mission as a Christian parent, what would you say? Read the following verses: Ephesians 4:11-16, Galatians 6:9-10, Deuteronomy 6:1-25, Acts 20:24.
2. What obstacles affect your mission now? What obstacles will affect your mission in the future?
3. What are your resources as a parent? How will you use them to continue your mission?

Passage III

Accept Your Assignment

"For our appeal does not spring from error or impurity or any attempt to deceive, but just as we have been approved by God to be entrusted with the gospel, so we speak, not to please man, but to please God who tests our hearts."
—I Thessalonians 2:3-4

God is at work calling out and transforming a people who will bear the likeness of his Son and enjoy God forever.

God's gracious plan is multi-generational, and the approved agents are parents who have been entrusted with the gospel.

We are charged with implementing God's plan, not our own.

The gospel is not only the beginning point to the Christian life, but it is the means for bringing us to our eternal destination.

Chapter 7

From Generation to Generation

A few years ago, we built a farmhouse on family land to provide a warm and inviting place for family and ministry opportunities. We incorporated several beautiful old doors salvaged from a 1920s local church.

When you walk through the church doors into the foyer of our farmhouse, you immediately see a large gold gilded frame. On the canvas, an Old Testament verse is written in a lovely calligraphy font.

"Tell it to your children, and let your children tell it to their children, and their children to the next generation" (Joel 1:3, NIV).

This verse from the prophet Joel serves as our farmhouse theme. It is a constant reminder of our desire to instill in our children and grandchildren such a love for God that it carries on from generation to generation.

Through his prophet, God warns the people about invasions of locusts and the need for future generations to recall this amazing event. To us, it is the perfect charge to not only tell our children about the God of the universe, but to strengthen them to stand strong in the face of adversity.

In Exodus 3:15, God tells Moses, "Say this to the people of Israel: 'The Lord, the God of your fathers, the God of Abraham, the God of Isaac, and the God of Jacob, has sent me to you.' This is my name forever, and thus I am to be remembered throughout all generations."

Throughout the Bible, we are instructed to remember God and his works and promises and pass them on to generations following us.

The message we sometimes hear is parents have little effect on shaping their children's moral and religious convictions. It is usually expressed as *No matter what parents do children will make up their own minds.*

But the reality is children *will* be shaped. In the absence of direction from parents, *someone* will shape their thinking. In the absence of understanding their origin, the meaning of their life, and their destiny, they will acquire a story from others who surround them or make one up.

In every instance, they are trying to make sense of it all.

Have you ever tried to put together a jigsaw puzzle without first seeing the picture on the box?

During the eighteen or so years your children are in your home, they will be handed many puzzles pieces. Some will be easy to fit together, some will be confusing and challenging. In the absence of a picture on the box (the big picture of God's eternal plan for the world and where they fit) your children will be lost in knowing how to assemble the pieces.

By the time they leave your care and start their own family, your children should know how the pieces of this life fit together. You will have been to them the picture on the box.

Consider this insightful quote from John Piper: "God does not drop a new Bible from heaven on every generation. He intends that the older generation will teach the newer generation to read and think and trust and obey and rejoice.

God draws personally near to every new generation of believers, but he does so through the truth they learn from preceding generations. The Spirit comes down vertically where the truth of God is imparted horizontally."[1]

If the truth is imparted horizontally, how many generations down the road do you desire to affect?

Consider and Apply:

1. Read Psalm 145:1-7. Paraphrase these verses in your own words.
2. Are you parenting for your great-grandchildren? What do you want to pass on to your children and their children's children and to the next generations?
3. We cannot pass on something we do not possess ourselves. If God's plan is multi-generational, what must be in place in your life to pass on convictions to your children and generations to follow? Consider these words from Alistair Begg: "A Christian way of thinking is not just thinking Christian thoughts, singing Christian songs, reading Christian books...; it is learning to think about the whole spectrum of life from the perspective of a mind that has been trained in truth."[2]

Chapter 8

Congratulations!
The Job is Yours!

One of our favorite books for children is *Flap Your Wings* by P.D. Eastman. In this insightful story, an egg mysteriously appears in Mr. and Mrs. Bird's nest. Though they are unsure if it is their egg, they determine to care for it to the best of their ability. "If an egg is in your nest, you sit on it and keep it warm," Mr. Bird says.

When the egg hatches and a baby alligator pops out, Mrs. Bird is not sure this is their baby at all. But Mr. Bird says, "He's in our nest, so he must be ours. His mouth is open so he must be hungry. When your baby is hungry, you feed him."

They work themselves to exhaustion feeding the alligator worms and bugs—lots of them! When the baby outgrows the nest, Mr. and Mrs. Bird encourage him to flap his wings and fly away.

Of course, Junior cannot fly and falls down, down, into the pond below. Mrs. Bird does not think Junior is a bird after all. As they watch him in the water, Mr. Bird proudly exclaims, "It doesn't matter. Just look at him swim!"[1]

When our first son was born, we felt a bit like Mr. and Mrs. Bird. He rocked our world as we knew it. In an instant, our lives of graduate school, work, trips with friends, concerts, and independence were replaced with a full-time, every waking moment, parenting role—one we certainly wanted and anticipated, but one we felt ill-equipped to fulfill.

If being a parent for the first time was not stressful enough, our little human suffered from colic which resulted in the three of us enduring many sleepless nights. Rocking, walking, rubbing his tummy--we repeated this same sequence hour after hour.

Did we feel inadequate and exhausted like Mr. and Mrs. Bird? Absolutely!

We're not sure which one of us thought, and possibly said aloud, "Are we sure this is our baby?" Of course, he was! But our sense of inadequacy caused doubt in our ability to be the parents God wanted us to be.

Were we prepared for this? The short answer is yes!

"But just as we have been approved by God to be entrusted with the gospel, so we speak, not to please man, but to please God who tests our hearts" (I Thessalonians 2:4). There is much to learn from this verse.

First of all, *you* have been approved by God to raise this child, this unique human. In being approved, you have been found worthy and adequate by the God who chose you. You have been authorized, affirmed, sanctioned.

In addition to being approved, God has equipped you with a natural affection for your children and a desire for their physical care. Besides your desire to protect and nurture, you have a desire to train them and pass on a culture.

God has provided a means for parents to grow in wisdom by giving us his Word and the Holy Spirit to guide us. Most importantly, God has entrusted Christian parents with the gospel which alone has the enduring power to bring about spiritual growth and life change.

God's multi-generational plan tells us we are entrusted with our children to not only physically care for them but to introduce them to Christ. We are to demonstrate how to be reconciled to God and model how to know and love him...for the preserving of the faith.

Consider and Apply:

1. Have you had thoughts of inadequacy when it comes to parenting? Where do you find your strength to continue in your parenting journey? See Psalm 73:26, Isaiah 12:2, Philippians 4:13, I Timothy 1:12.

2. Consider this quote by Douglas Wilson. "Good parents are instructed by God to prepare their children to leave at the proper time...Parents bring up their children to be colonists at the proper time, planting families of their own."[2] What steps will you take now to prepare your children to leave the nest and plant families of their own?

Chapter 9

Investing the Good News

When we speak of having something entrusted to us, we do not think of frivolous things but rather something of real value. If someone of high authority entrusted us with something of value to pass on to someone they dearly loved, a sense of extreme urgency and care would attend our delivery.

Whether monetary aid, food and shelter, or a life-saving medicine, we would be motivated in our efforts by a sense of obligation and love. In a way, we would be in debt to the recipients until we delivered.

With our thirteen grandchildren, we desired to illustrate how sharing gifts entrusted to us transfers blessing. Like all of us, they will have the opportunity to pursue a life of seeking to entertain themselves with pleasures or be engaged in using their gifts to serve others.

One path will lead them on a never-ending quest that will only bring unfulfilled pursuits. The selfless path will bring true happiness and fulfillment. When we look five or ten years down the road, what do we hope to see in their lives? I Peter 4:10 says, "As each has received a gift, use it to serve one another, as good stewards of God's varied grace."

To demonstrate this concept, we launched "The Stewardship Project" by giving each child a monetary gift. Whenever we give money for a birthday gift, it is given without conditions or instructions for how to invest it. This time, the gift was given with one condition—to bless others.

As stewards of the money, they determined how to use it for the common good. The children could hardly wait to bless someone with the gift they had received. They felt a sense of obligation and even urgency to deliver the money to someone in need.

Similarly, the gospel has come to us as a gift; we have no liberty to keep it for ourselves nor to dawdle in our delivery mission. Lifesaving news is for sharing and we are under obligation to make it known to others, especially to our children.

The Apostle Paul felt this urgency. In Romans 1:14, Paul says he is obligated. "I am under obligation." Paul considered himself to be in debt to both the Romans and the entire Gentile world. Jesus Christ had entrusted him with the gospel for them.

Paul wrote, "So I am eager to preach the gospel to you also who are in Rome" (Romans 1:15).

God has entrusted us with something of great value to deliver to our children. He has invited us to participate in a Stewardship Project with eternal significance—to share the good news of Jesus with them.

We know we have rightly communicated the message of Christ to our young children if they hear, "Jesus welcomes you. Come and follow him." When we see them respond with a desire to come to Jesus and follow him, we know they understand.

To older children who have chosen a different path, the message is the same. "Come and follow Jesus." In their case, like the prodigal, this may involve turning and returning. The message is still a tender, "Come and be welcomed by Jesus."

Consider and Apply:

1. Read Romans 1:14-15. Why was Paul eager to preach the gospel? Do you find yourself eager to share the good news of Jesus Christ? If good news is for sharing, what keeps us from confidently speaking about what we know to be true?
2. How could you utilize a stewardship project with your children? What lessons might be learned?

Passage IV

Shepherd With Your Words

"For we never came with words of flattery, as you know, nor with a pretext for greed—God is witness. Nor did we seek glory from people, whether from you or from others, though we could have made demands as apostles of Christ."

—I Thessalonians 2:5-6

The Christian life is a ministry of words and service. This is certainly true of our ministry as parents.

Paul mentions his words of wisdom, affirmation, and hope--words not to please men but God.

Though Paul exhorts, he is gentle and affectionate.

Our integrity gives respect and strength to our words, resulting in our children's growth in faith and character.

Chapter 10

Words Matter

Even though we understand our place as change agents in our children's lives, we often feel stuck in everyday management, instruction, and correction. When our children are young, we typically cover the same material over and over again, making it feel like a daily version of "yakety-yak."

In an informal poll, we asked a group of parents of young children what the most wearisome part of parenting was. Nearly every one of them said: *repetition.* Some added: *without seeing results.* Their responses brought back memories.

With four young boys in our home, one of them could not walk through the living room without getting hit by a flying object, tripped, or wrestled to the floor. The question, "Why did you hit (trip, pinch, tackle) your brother?" was not just asked once then put to rest for life. It was addressed hundreds of times.

The commitment we made when our sons were first placed in our arms kept us from losing heart—the commitment to shape not only their behavior but the thinking which gives rise to their behavior. Awareness of our child's sin was no accident. It was an opportunity. Grace can only be made visible as a response to failure.

In the "Parenting with Mercy" interview on FamilyLife Today, Paul David Tripp discussed a parent's commitment to their children and said the following...

"Understand largely, change is a process, not an event. God called me...to commit myself to 10,000 conversations, 10,000 moments...Let me say it this way...I think this is so important to get hold of.

If your eyes ever see and your ears ever hear the sin, weakness, and failure of your children, it's never an accident, it's never an interruption, it's never a hassle--it's always grace. God loves that child. He has put him in a family of faith, and He will reveal the need of that child to you so you can be God's tool of redemptive rescue and help. That's parenting!"[1]

This is played out most profoundly in our own homes. Our children will struggle with sin throughout their entire life. What opportunities has God given us?

We are there along the way during their childhood, through 10,000 plus conversations, to be God's tool of redemptive rescue and help. As Christian parents, our desire is to make the unseen God visible. With our words, we have an opportunity to paint the picture of Jesus and show our children the beauty of God.

If we desire to instruct our children and draw them to Christ, the tone of our words must be as purposeful as the words themselves. All humans are naturally reactive. If someone snaps at us, we tend to snap back. This is our protective instinct.

Our words of instruction to our children will be ineffective if the tone and temperature are not right. Think of tone and temperature as reagents; something added to our words to enhance their effect. Humans react best to warmth displayed in kindness and gentleness. Our words and how we use them matter!

Consider and Apply:

1. Do you speak so as to please God? What would it look like to speak and parent so as to please man?
2. Did you experience verbal interactions last week that did not go well? If you had an audio recording of a conversation, what would it reveal?
3. Rate your percentage of time listening to your children versus talking. Compare the two. Does something need to change to improve the communication between you and your children?
4. All children, especially teenagers, tend to hear criticism in our instruction and interrogation in our questions. They perceive our words as implying they need to adjust something to conform to our standard. Observe and read your child's responses to your words.

Resources:

- Paul David Tripp, *Parenting: 14 Gospel Principles That Can Radically Change Your Family* (Wheaton, Illinois: Crossway, 2016)

Chapter 11

The Power of Validation

As we see in Paul's letter to the Thessalonians, he continually uplifted his spiritual children with encouraging words. Paul acknowledged their situations, identifying and empathizing with them.

Not words of flattery. Not words to coddle their ears. Nor words telling them only what they wanted to hear.

He did not speak from selfishness, nor to seek glory. Well then, you might ask, what did he say? Clearly, he pastored and shepherded. Parents, what do *your* sheep need? More often than not, they tell you. However, our responses may be so automatic we do not really hear them. Consider the typical parent responses:

I'm scared. (That's silly. You have nothing to be afraid of.)

I'm sad. (You shouldn't be sad!)

I'm angry. (You have no reason to be angry.)

I'm dumb. (Of course, you're not!)

Most parents have probably heard it all and said it all. When we hear a child expressing these thoughts and feelings, our natural inclination is to contradict and quickly correct them. Or just get the child to stop crying and listen.

After all, we need to make the bus, get to church on time, go to bed, or a host of other pressing matters. These responses are more natural to us than pausing to validate their feelings because our own feelings tend to complicate the situation.

Dictionaries define validation as recognition or affirmation that a person, their feelings, or opinions are valid or worthwhile. Think *acknowledgment*. Acknowledging a child's thoughts and feelings, acknowledging they are true and real to *them* regardless of logic.

"Regardless of logic" may be the key words here. The feelings may not make sense to anyone else. To a child, acknowledging translates to understanding. It means parents keep their desire to instruct in check until the child's emotions subside. Though emotions can lead to sinful behavior, they are not sinful.

They are natural.

In *Loving the Little Years: Motherhood in the Trenches*, author Rachel Janovic describes our children's emotions as spirited horses. She understands her task as a parent is to teach the young riders how to manage their horses. A spirited horse tends to run away with us—a frightening experience.

If this happens, your child may feel a loss of control. The goal is not to cripple the horse but to equip the rider.[1] A wise parent knows how to validate the emotions and give the grace of time for the child to pull back on the reins before proceeding with instruction.

This idea of validation has been recognized in the world of clinical psychology for many years. Psychologists found when they immediately attempted to solve their client's life problems, their client's emotions became more intense.

By first communicating to a client their thoughts and concerns were understood, emotions lessened, and the session could continue in a more positive way. For parents, validating means letting children share their thoughts and feelings without judging, criticizing, ridiculing, or abandoning them.[2]

In considering what validation is, we must also understand what it is not. Validating your child's emotions is not permissiveness. A parent can validate a child's feeling of frustration with a friend while also communicating hitting the friend is wrong.

Validation is not the same as encouraging and praising. We praise our children for playing well in a sporting event. We validate their feelings when they struggle with not playing as well as they wanted to. Validation is not necessarily showing agreement with nor approval of what they are saying, just that you understand what they are feeling.

Validation is not a new concept. A wise King Solomon said. "A word fitly spoken is like apples of gold in a setting of silver. Like a gold ring or an ornament of gold is a wise reprover to a listening ear" (Proverbs 25:11-12). What does King Solomon mean by "fitly spoken"? The words *purposely spoken* come to mind. "Apples of gold in a setting of silver" creates an image of loveliness and comfort.

Validation is all about the right word at the right time.

Consider and Apply:

1. Read Psalm 46:1. God invites us to bring our emotions to him. He is our refuge. Our tendency is to not welcome our children until they get their emotions under control. How can you respond as an emotional refuge to your children?
2. What does scripture have to say about our words? What are specific strategies for talking to our children and acknowledging their feelings, fears, and concerns? See Proverbs 16:21-24.
3. Awareness is the first step to changing parenting behavior that can have long-reaching implications for your child's emotional growth. Be present for your children and listen intently to what they say. Help them articulate their feelings. When emotions are high, validate. Do not try to solve right away. Validation will become more natural over time!

Resources:

- Rachel Janovic, *Loving the Little Years: Motherhood in the Trenches* (Moscow, Idaho: Canon Press, 2010)
- Karyn D. Hall and Melissa H. Cook, *The Power of Validation* (New Harbinger Publications, 2011)

Chapter 12

Hope Protects and Makes the Heart Glad

Every year as soon as the Christmas tree is packed away, our thirteen grandchildren embark on what we call Table Rock Talk. All twenty-three of us consider our annual July vacation to this beautiful lake in Missouri one of the highlights of our year. Since our marriage in 1972, we have gone to Table Rock Lake with the Schuermann family every single summer.

When we sadly say goodbye to the lake at the end of our vacation, we anticipate returning the following July. We anticipate it *and* we have hope for our return. However, as much as we love our vacation, we are realistic enough to know something might happen to change our plans for the following year—an unexpected illness, change in resort ownership, or even a global pandemic.

By God's grace, our family will journey back to Table Rock Lake the next year...and the next.

Throughout the Bible, God is presented as the God of Hope for those who trust in him. Hope in

God involves believing promises which are far more certain than anything else we might put our hope in.

In Hebrew, hope is the word *tikvah* (teek-VAH). *Strong's Concordance* defines it as an expectation and trust, waiting for something to come. The word comes from the Hebrew root *kavah* which also means to bind together as in a cord or a rope.[1]

This creates a strong visual of something we not only see but hold on to as a rock climber clings to a rope securely attached to the destination.

In Hebrews 6:19, hope is called the anchor of the soul because it gives stability to the Christian life. But hope is not simply wishful thinking; rather, it is that which latches on to the certainty of God's promises for our future. In his commentary on Romans 8, Dr. R.C. Sproul says "Hope is not taking a deep breath and *hoping* things are going to turn out all right. It is assurance that God is going to do what he says he will do." [2]

Sproul explains hope is about a destination and it lifts our gaze to the future. Hope involves a desire we will arrive in a better place. It lifts us above the distress or unpleasantness of the now and brings us to anticipate and also labor toward what will be better. Without it, men despair.

Believing God and holding on to the "rope of hope" can be great encouragement to the mature.

The psalmists, after lamenting their present difficulties, turned to praising God and expressing trust in his promises. The apostles also continually encouraged people about a future hope and a future inheritance. Though we can find great encouragement here, looking past the situations of today can be difficult. No person who has ever lived has escaped disappointment. And no person has escaped the need to have hope.

What does this mean for our children? Hope is especially abstract for kids as they typically live in a world of now. They want the hope of a better tomorrow, not necessarily of a better eternity.

Trusting in the future God promises does not make sense to them when it is all about "I didn't make the team." Lamentations 3:21 says, "But this I call to mind, and therefore I have hope."

Speaking words children can call to mind, grounded in biblical truth and reality, will take our children from despair, from thinking there is no way out, to a desire to continue on. Hope is the way forward.

When our children feel stuck, when they feel devalued, guilty, lonely, or afraid, they must have something to hold on to. They need to hear words of hope on many occasions and from many sources, but especially from their parents.

Paul often assured his spiritual children they were very dear to him. Did those words give them hope in God? Without a doubt. So, gather your children in your arms and bless them with assurance.

- *I love you. You are so dear to me.*
- *Being with you makes my heart happy.*
- *God loves our family, and he is preparing a place for us where everything will be made right one day.*

- *I understand your disappointment (anger, sadness, frustration). You are no less important to me because of it.*
- *Let's pray about this and work together.*

For hope to be more than wishful thinking, it must be secured by genuine words of what God has promised. These promises are only as sure as the trustworthiness of the promisor and his ability to deliver. Parents are the vehicle for transferring this to their children.

What is your rope of hope secured to?

Consider and Apply:

1. Read Romans 8:24-25. Describe the difference between hope and wishful thinking. How do you model this and explain it to your children?
2. In *Mere Christianity*, C.S. Lewis wrote: "[Hope] means that a continual looking forward to the eternal world...is not a form of escapism or wishful thinking, but one of the things a Christian is meant to do. It does not require us to leave the world as it is. If you read history, you will find that the Christians who did the most for this present world were those who thought the most of the next."[3]
3. Read I Peter 3:15, II Peter 3:13, Psalm 121. How do you demonstrate the "hope that is within you?"

sharing common traits of gentleness, affection, wisdom, and a desire to sacrificially give of themselves to their families.

In describing his ministry in I Thessalonians 2:7-8, Paul likens himself to a mother in the gentleness and affection he displayed toward them. He says, like a mother, he and his ministry team were ready to share the gospel of God, to impart truth and wisdom, and to lay out their lives for the benefit of their spiritual children.

In his commentary on these verses, John Calvin says, "A mother with her children manifests a rare and wonderful affection toward her children. She spares no labor and trouble, shuns no anxiety, works tirelessly, and even with cheerfulness of spirit gives her own self."[3]

If you read Proverbs 31:10-31, you will see the character traits Paul describes and more. You read about how women are to be praised and honored for their character and noble works. The words detail the mother's gentleness and affection as she extends her hand to the poor and reaches out her hands to the needy.

They tell of her words of truth and how she opens her mouth with wisdom. The teaching of kindness is on her tongue. She is a hard worker, looking to the ways of her household and avoiding the bread of idleness.

Some think of the Proverbs 31 woman as an unrealistic example, even unattainable. But these verses are not meant to be a "to do" list for women

Passage V

Embrace Motherhood

"But we were gentle among you, like a nursing mother taking care of her own children.
So, being affectionately desirous of you, we were ready to share with you not only the gospel of God but also our own selves, because you have become very dear to us."
—I Thessalonians 2:7-8

Mothers are gifted by God for their important work with their families and the world beyond.

One of their most joyful opportunities is shaping and influencing young daughters as they grow to embrace godly womanhood.

Another fulfilling opportunity is found in raising sons to embrace biblical manhood and become men of virtue.

Chapter 13

The Gift of Mothers

The remarkable characteristics of mothers are universally recognized, to the point of being humorous. These traits were also recognized by our sons who often wondered, *How did she know? Does she have eyes in the back of her head?*

In *Eve in Exile and the Restoration of Femininity*, author Rebekah Merkle asks, "So, what are we designed to be? What are the problems for which we are the solutions? Of course, in a godless universe we were not designed for anything…but then again, we do not live in that world. We live in a world God designed on purpose, and he had certain things in mind as he did so."[1]

God created woman to be the solution for blessing mankind, the perfect partner for Adam in reigning over the earth, cultivating and filling it. As Merkle says, Adam alone is just Adam. Adam with Eve…becomes the human race.[2]

Every gift from God is given for the common good, for the blessing of humankind. We see these extraordinary gifts in the day-to-day lives of millions upon millions of mothers around the world, all

or to instill any sense of guilt. Remember, not every mom needs to buy and sell land, plant a vineyard, and make her family's clothing.

Set your guilt aside!

This section of Scripture is designed to point out the gifts God gave to woman when he created her and what those may look like with her family. Note the introduction and you will see it was written by a man, King Lemuel. In these verses, he details what his mother taught him about women.

Proverbs 31 was not written as a handbook for women. It was written for husbands, fathers, and children to understand the wonderful gift they have been given.

Consider and Apply:

1. Often motherhood includes the "guilt that keeps on giving." Why do moms struggle with guilt? How can they learn to see themselves as God sees them?
2. One of the most important things fathers can do is to love their wives passionately, faithfully, unreservedly. Dads, how do you support your wife in motherhood? Do you "praise her in the gates" before your children and others?
3. Many forces are at work to distract women from enjoying and administering their gifts. Embrace your value as a mom. Recognize and celebrate the God-given gifts in yourself and in your daughters.

Resources:

- Rebekah Merkle, *Eve in Exile and the Restoration of Femininity* (Moscow, Idaho: Canon Press, 2016)

Chapter 14

Mothers and Daughters

When we think about illustrations of everyday life, we nearly always come to Norman Rockwell, the great American painter and illustrator. Over a span of forty-seven years, he depicted almost every aspect of family life and made people around the world smile.

On a Saturday Evening Post cover published in 1954, Rockwell thoughtfully captured an adolescent girl as she studies herself in the mirror. The painting is called "Girl at Mirror."[1] You can easily find the image on the internet. It is worth finding for Rockwell deftly painted the world of this young girl, filling it with insightful and symbolic elements.

A glamor magazine lays open on the girl's lap as she ponders herself in the mirror. Note the doll, representing the natural play of younger girls, now tossed aside. A tube of red lipstick, a brush and comb are ready to be taken up, to transform her into a beauty.

Yet, she looks apprehensive rather than confident. Is she nervous about the transition from girl to young woman? It isn't hard to imagine the questions she may have. *Who will I be? Will people like me? Will I find happiness? Will I be as lovely as the woman in the magazine?*

In any young girl's world, many voices and spokesmodels offer to help. Imagine her searching for answers to these questions from the world of the media, glamour images, and friends.

For your daughters, these are not just whimsical daydreams but very weighty questions. They do want to be liked, they want to be valued, and they want to find happiness. The answers to your daughters' questions can lead them to hope or to despair. Visualize the same girl with an open Bible on her lap and with a wise mother guiding her to ask the right questions.

- *Who am I? Who was I created to be?*
- *Do I have value?*
- *Who can help me find happiness?*
- *How can I know what is right and what is wrong?*
- *What is the meaning of my life?*
- *How can I best use my gifts?*

In *Raising a Strong Daughter in a Toxic Culture: 11 Steps to Keep Her Happy, Healthy, and Safe*, author and pediatrician Meg Meeker distinguishes the difference between modeling and mentoring.

Moms are always modeling.

They do it every day without even thinking about it. "Mentoring, on the other hand, is about consciously, openly teaching daughters about life. Part of it is still teaching by example, but much of it is teaching by discussion or instruction."[2] Mentoring takes modeling to a different, more intellectual level.

Mothers are to provide their young girls with the truth about who God made them to be. This responsibility cannot be overstated. Through purposeful conversations, mothers can celebrate their daughters' gifts and lead them to the opportunities God has given them for fulfillment. By guiding their daughters to ask the *right* questions, mothers can help direct them to the right answers.

Consider and Apply:

1. What is the difference between modeling and mentoring? What do you do well and where could you improve?

2. "Daughters see their mothers as offering security, comfort, dependability, and love, and if that relationship is strong, she will hold her mother closer than her most devoted friend"[3] (Meeker). Imagine you are standing before a mirror contemplating what your daughter sees as she looks at you. What actions do you need to take to support your daughter's image of you as a follower of Christ?

3. Read Psalm 119:73, Psalm 139:13-14, Philippians 1:6, II Timothy 1:7. How do you direct your daughter to ask the right questions?

4. Pray faithfully for your daughters and granddaughters. Pray they would...

   - learn from strong, capable women who fear God.
   - see their own character qualities and strengths as God's design.
   - use their strengths in virtuous ways to glorify God and serve others.

Resources:

- Meg Meeker, M.D., *Raising a Strong Daughter in a Toxic Culture: 11 Steps to Keep Her Happy, Healthy, and Safe* (Regnery Publishing, 2020)

Chapter 15

Mothers and Sons

Our sons are grown men now, but I (Cheryl) remember the early years vividly. Four boys in less than seven years made our home a very active place, indeed. You can imagine the extent of our interactions in one day.

I was busy. They were busy.

We were always doing something fun together—mostly outside. Hiking, fishing, picking blackberries, catching critters, and turning every roasting pan I ever owned into a terrarium.

Recognizing their strengths and voicing those strengths to my boys came easy. I recall discussing the Ten to One Rule with friends: ten compliments to one criticism. However, as many moms experience, I also found it easy to fall into patterns of scolding when addressing wrongdoing—especially when one or more boys were arguing or wailing.

On the way home from a wonderful vacation several years ago, Stan and I read Emerson Eggerichs' book, *Mother and Son: The Respect Effect*. Eggerichs is an internationally known author and public speaker on the topic of male-female relationships and family dynamics. He is the author of the marriage book, *Love and Respect: The Love She Most Desires; The Respect He Desperately Needs.*

In *Mother and Son: The Respect Effect*, the author notes some women who attended his marriage conferences asked an interesting question. If respect works on the masculine souls of husbands, would it also work on the masculine souls of sons? Many women tried it with their boys and wrote Eggerichs with testimonies about how their relationships with their sons had improved and, in some cases, were transformed. Moms wrote about their sons from four-year-old boys to teens to adults.

In his research, the author discovered little or no reference to the words respect or honor in popular books about raising boys. He found little about how boys need to feel respected for who they are as "men in the making."

In his many conversations with mothers, he also discovered mothers coached their husbands on how to love their daughters, but no one was teaching moms how to respect their sons. While most mothers are tuned in to the nurturing and love aspects of mothering sons, many may not intentionally think about their son's need for respect.

What does respect look like with a mother and son? The author suggests a mother should express respectful words toward her son, no matter what he does.

Even when he is being disobedient? Yes!

Her son may not deserve respect at that moment, but he will not respond to negativity and disrespect in the long term. Instead, he may resist or rebel against what he sees as his mother's disapproval.

What does this look like when a son is disobedient? The author says it will look one of two ways: "Either a mother will show respect and positive regard toward the spirit of her son while confronting his wrongdoing, or she will show disrespect and negative regard toward the spirit of her son while confronting his sinful choices. There is no third option."[1]

A mother can be angry about the choices her son makes and have plans for discipline. At the same time, she can express respect for the person God is making him to be. "I do not respect your wrong choices, and you will be disciplined for them…[but] I respect the person God is making you to be and we will get through this moment."[2] The author calls this *unconditional positive regard* which does not come naturally to any of us.[3]

For those of you who are boy moms, there is much to digest here. Like men, boys filter their world through a respect grid; merely the appearance of disrespect can be enough to derail a relationship.

Moms naturally default to love and hugs but may have to consciously think about showing respect to their sons in meaningful ways. It is our task and responsibility to parent with their needs in mind.

Consider and Apply:

1. Boys filter their world through the respect grid. Can you identify times when your son(s) appeared to tune you out? How could this new understanding help you heal the relationship?
2. How can you begin to show respect and positive regard toward your son while, at the same time, confronting his wrongdoing? Read Proverbs 15:1, 4; 16:24; 18:4.
3. Consider this quote by Douglas Wilson. "Faith is central in bringing up boys, but it is important to remember that the object of faith is not the boy. It is faith in God, faith in his promises, faith in his wisdom…Parents are to believe God *for* their sons, which is a very different thing than believing *in* their sons."[4]
4. As you make changes in how you interact with your son, note the difference in his responses over time. Rejoice in your improved relationship with your son.

Resources:

- Emerson Eggerichs, Mother *and Son: The Respect Effect* (Thomas Nelson, 2016)
- Douglas Wilson, *Future Men: Raising Boys to Fight Giants* (Canon Press, 2016)
- Meg Meeker, M.D., *Strong Mothers, Strong Sons* (Ballantine Books, 2015)

Passage VI

Love and Live the Upright Life

"For you remember, brothers, our labor and toil: we worked night and day, that we might not be a burden to any of you, while we proclaimed to you the gospel of God. You are witnesses, and God also, how holy and righteous and blameless was our conduct toward you believers."

—I Thessalonians 2:9-10

Who we are with our children is of utmost importance.

We are always teaching because our children are always witnessing our behavior.

By our lives, we either validate or contradict the truth we claim to believe.

Chapter 16

Creating Culture

When Christian parents hear "the culture" they often think about ways to build "Fort Family" to keep their kids protected inside and keep the culture outside. Though the word is used frequently, looking more closely at the etymology gives us insight.

By Merriam-Webster's definition, culture is a compilation of the characteristic features of everyday existence and a pattern of behavior shared by people in a place or time. It comes from a French word derived from the Latin "colere" which means to tend the earth, cultivate, and actively foster growth.

From the moment Adam and Eve were given dominion over the earth, the question has been...

What will people do with their world?

Though scripture does not use the term *culture*, it does instruct us about the life that creates it. What we do (our conduct) and what we say (our words) in our home create patterns that not only affect those inside of our home but those in the community beyond our walls.

Douglas Wilson writes, "Children should view the home as not simply the place where they eat and sleep, but where they are taught and shaped. They should view home as the center of their world. They should see it as their primary culture—and always view the larger culture in the light of what they have learned at home."[1]

Paul had a vision for seeing Christ honored everywhere, but his immediate focus was on the culture inside of the churches which he described as the household of God (Ephesians 2:19). He continually labored to build households of believers who were of the same mind, worshipped the same Lord, and demonstrated the working of the Holy Spirit in their lives.

He desired they would grow up together and their God-honoring culture and virtues would eventually influence the world outside. "I, therefore, a prisoner for the Lord, urge you to walk in a manner worthy of the calling to which you have been called" (Ephesians 4:1).

Christian parents are called to create the same environment in their homes. In their comprehensive guide concerning culture and its effects, *A Practical Guide to Culture: Helping the Next Generation Navigate Today's World*, authors John Stonestreet and Brett Kunkle address this very topic.

"We must make sure our kids understand Christian faith as more than a set of beliefs and behaviors. Instead, they need to know that a competing vision of life demands their deepest allegiance and grounds their identity.

After all, the question is how they'll respond when the cultural pressure is *really* on. Will they do what is right even when all of the incentives promote doing wrong? Will they recognize the lies and still embrace what is true?

And will they not only survive the culture but also be able to engage it with courage, clarity, and resolve, standing for Christ wherever He has placed them and in whatever work He has called them to?"[2]

Great questions! All of us acknowledge the importance of creating a godly culture in our homes. This task will take commitment, diligence, and much reliance on God's wisdom to see our children flourish as we so fervently desire.

Consider and Apply:

1. What does the culture in your home look like? How would an observer describe it? "After all, culture's greatest influence is in what it presents as being normal"[3] (Stonestreet and Kunkle).

2. In the Bible, "the world" represents mankind's attempt at using and enjoying all things apart from God's design (See Romans 12:1-2). How are we to live in the physical world but live differently from what it represents?

3. In a message titled, "The Church in Your House," Charles Spurgeon shares a vision of how we should understand the culture in our home. "If there is such a Church in our house, let us order it well, and let everyone conduct themselves as in the sight of God. Let us go about our daily routines with studied holiness, diligence, kindness, and integrity. More is expected of a Church than of an ordinary household. Family worship must, in such a case, be more devout and heartier; internal love must be warmer and unbroken, and external conduct must be more sanctified and Christlike."[4]

Resources:

- John Stonestreet and Brett Kunkel, *A Practical Guide to Culture: Helping the Next Generation*

Navigate Today's World (Colorado Springs, CO: David C. Cook, 2017)

Chapter 17

A Family That Works

My mother (Stan) was a keen observer of people and of families. She was careful to not criticize others, though when she saw something in a family that encouraged her, she might say, "that family just works."

We knew what she meant. She had observed something in the family's conduct. Maybe it was individually, or it could have been collectively, but she saw something unique. The family obviously had an effect on her. In her mind, the family worked as intended.

Think about your family. Would others say, "Wow, that family works!"

In the 21st century, we live in a world surrounded by many conveniences. All need to work properly to be helpful. Everything that does not work as designed is merely a source of frustration and can even be counter-productive.

Anyone who has ever tried to fix an appliance or machine first hopes they will find the coveted "reset button." God created marriage and the family with a designed purpose. If your family does not seem to be working, you may be on the verge of yelling...

"Reset! Reset!"

God's plan for the family is in many ways the same as his plan for the church. In his letter to the Ephesians, Paul describes the church as God's household (Ephesians 2:19). Paul says when the church functions properly, each member of the household will grow up to maturity (Ephesians 4:16). Additionally, each contributes their individual gifts for the common good, thus ensuring the building up of the entire body (family).

Throughout his letters, Paul gives instruction on how the churches are to work properly. Here are some examples:

- Does each member have a proper attitude of contentment? (I Thessalonians 5:16-18)
- Are they engaged in good deeds? (Titus 3:14)
- Do they view others with respect and speak accordingly? (Ephesians 4:29)
- Are some members over-committed and producing an excess of busyness? (I Thessalonians 4:11-12)
- Are members stimulated by the right things? (Philippians 4:8)
- Are they absorbing too many outside influences? (Romans 12:2)

The Christian family is designed to help each individual flourish and grow up. Paul describes the upright life as holy, righteous, and blameless, all characteristics observable by our conduct. We are to guide each member of the family toward maturity, understanding they have different needs, traits, and gifts. Are you a family that works?

Consider and Apply:

1. Consider what Jesus says about the need for rest (Mark 6:31). One opportunity families have to reset is during dinnertime. How could you use this time to focus on those topics critical to growing up?

2. Many adults did not experience a family committed to living within God's design. Even as adults with children of their own, they may desire to change the way their family now operates. To these parents, we would say, "Begin where you are and start a new branch on the tree."

3. Read Titus 2:14, 3:8. Paul says we were purified for a purpose. What is this purpose? How does this encourage you to create a culture in your home that pursues ways to bless others? How can you be good stewards of the gifts you have been given?

4. As Christians, we are called to model a different way of living on this earth. What does this mean to you and your family?

Chapter 18

When Sin Looks Abnormal

Do you know how agents are trained to recognize counterfeit currency? They are trained in the authentic. Agents cannot be trained in all the various kinds of counterfeits as there are far too many. They memorize the face of the true. This illustration has often been used to show how Christians gain discernment in identifying what is true and what is false.

Christian author Tim Challis was curious enough to verify the idea for himself. He made an appointment with the Bank of Canada and interviewed an agent who did indeed verify this is the training their agents receive.

To test the process, Challies received a brief training on the marks of authentic currency; he was given the opportunity to use his new skills on a variety of bills. With his understanding of the real, he was able to accurately spot and reject all of the false bills. He later used this illustration to speak to Christians about how they can discern and be protected from false doctrine.[1]

We can learn to spot the counterfeit but only if we know the authentic. In our world, counterfeiters are busy and creative, always coining some new way to deceive. All attempt to make their product look like the true currency.

The Bible identifies this masterful game of deception as *the world*. In the world, we and our children are offered alternatives to everything true and biblical--new lifestyles, new spirituality, and new morals.

In *Losing Our Virtue*, author David F. Wells says worldliness is what makes sin look normal...and righteousness look odd. Every one of us can immediately name several examples. He goes on to describe worldliness as "that system of values, in any given age, which has at its center our fallen human perspective, which displaces God and his truth from the world, and which makes sin look normal and righteousness seem strange. It thus gives great plausibility to what is morally wrong and, for that reason, makes what is wrong seem normal."[2]

If this is true, consider the counter statement: *In the light of a righteous life, sin will look abnormal.* These statements are profound with significant implications for our children.

How will we protect ourselves and our children in this world flooded in counterfeit values and morals and lifestyles? There is good news, for God has designed the family and the church to teach and trade with the authentic.

In doing this, we assure ourselves and our children the greatest blessings as they live according to what is true. Paul instructed his disciple, Timothy, to follow what he observed of Paul's teaching and life.

As he writes to Timothy, Paul mentions his conduct, his aim in life, his faith, his patience, his love, and his steadfastness. Can you imagine the value of observing such a godly man as Paul as he ministers to people? Timothy saw not only the authentic Christian life, but he also observed how Paul endured challenges and persecutions. See II Timothy 3:10-14.

It is in the church and in the family where our children learn about authentic marriage, hospitality, service, and love. The list is long. When your children go outside of your home, you want the sin they see to look odd and abnormal to them.

This will be their greatest protection. We want our children to resist temptation by knowing something better exists than what is presented to them. In I Thessalonians 5:21-22, Paul encourages his spiritual children to "test everything; hold fast what is good. Abstain from every form of evil."

Consider this quote from Tim Challies. "The more we know about God's character, God's ways, and God's Word, the greater the contrast will be between truth and error."[3]

Consider and Apply:

1. *The world* presents a way of thinking and living that is unbiblical, but its currency is designed to look like the true. How will you teach your children to value what is true and recognize the counterfeit?
2. Do your children have many opportunities to observe the authentic version of love, marriage, service and worship outside of the home? How will you increase these opportunities?
3. Read Romans 12:2. How will you apply this in your family?

Resources:

- David F. Wells, *Losing our Virtue* (Wm. B. Eerdmans Publishing Co., 1999)
- Tim Challies, https://www.challies.com/articles/counterfeit-detection-part-1/
- Tim Challies, https://www.challies.com/articles/counterfeit-detection-part-2/

Passage VII

Do Fatherhood the Right Way

"For you know how, like a father with his children,
we exhorted each one of you and encouraged you
and charged you..."
—I Thessalonians 2:11-12

Fathers are naturally given to instructing and
admonishing their children.

With this strength comes the potential of
exasperating our children if admonishment is
overbearing or harsh.

Our instruction must always be tempered with
tenderness and understanding, and a good dose of
fun!

Chapter 19

The Gift of Fathers

When Paul stated in I Thessalonians 2:11 that he acted like a father with his children, he chose three different words to describe his fatherly instruction to the church. He said he exhorted, encouraged, and charged them.

We recognize these characteristics since they are natural to a father. No one expects a father to be neglectful or indifferent to the upbringing of his children. Exhorting and encouraging and charging are what fathers are made to do.

We also understand the wisdom needed by our children can only come from the source of wisdom, which is God himself. To supply this, fathers must make regular excursions to the source in order to bring wise and tender words to their children.

In his plan for the family, God created fathers to guide, to watch over, to preserve and restore. This is not a burdensome task for the one who loves his children. He gladly expends himself for their sake.

Sacrificial duty is its own fulfillment.

Paul first mentions exhortation, which includes instruction and teaching. Dads are good at this one, aren't they? As we noted, it is natural. When giving exhortation, they have a destination or a character trait in mind for their children. Paul's exhortation was given so the Thessalonians would walk in a manner worthy of the God who calls them.

In the desire to shape their children and move them toward responsible adulthood, dads can easily exercise such a degree of control that the child loses heart. This can occur even though the intent is to instruct.

In Colossians 3:21, Paul cautions, "Fathers, do not provoke your children, lest they become discouraged." And, in Ephesians 6:4, "Fathers, do not provoke your children to anger, but bring them up in the discipline and instruction of the Lord."

Paul encourages restraint—being under control, within limits, moderate. Immoderate harshness can cause children to be so disheartened, they may be incapable of receiving any honorable training.

Our children need to be *encouraged*, thus Paul's second word.

When we think of encouraging our children, we realize there are many times when a wise father understands his children's need for assurance. They need to know Dad is listening to them. Our children often lack courage because they are growing up in a world increasingly hostile to them and their beliefs.

Dads, the best way to encourage your children to walk the worthy walk is to be with them on their journey to spiritual maturity. "Hey, walk with me. We will do this together."

If you have ever been assigned a task, you received a directive and were charged with completing a mission. Those in the military understand authority means having the ability to impose obligation.

Paul charged the Thessalonians to walk in a manner worthy of their calling. But his was not a "go and do" directive. Paul offered himself as an example, and most importantly, offered to "go and do" with them.

Here is the great opportunity given to fathers, to invite their children to walk with them. Going with them has much greater power for transforming lives than merely giving instructions. We have the opportunity to demonstrate and model our obedience and invite our children to join us.

We may think we have more power as drivers of our children, but we have more power as *draw-ers* of our children. Few people shape our character and our personality more than our father.

Fathers are not to indulge and spoil their children nor are they to humiliate and suppress them. The challenge in fatherhood is to get this right. "The righteous who walks in his integrity—blessed are his children after him!" (Proverbs 20:7)

Consider and Apply:

1. Being a father is a high and noble calling, and we understand our tendencies, good and bad. But let's consider how fathers can avoid doing the very thing Paul warns about in Colossians 3 and Ephesians 6. Note the ways Dads can exasperate their children, inspired by Alistair Begg.[1]

   - *Injustice.* Children know about fairness and have a strong internal sense of justice. Have you heard "That's not fair!" in your home?

   - *Inconsistency.* Children readily recognize inconsistency. They will notice every gap between Dad's words and Dad's life.

   - *Severity.* All discipline should be measured and meted out without anger. The punishment should fit the crime.

   - *Favoritism.* Think about favoritism as being kin to comparison. You may deny being guilty of favoritism, but what about comparison?

   - *Belittling achievements.* Comparison can come into play here. Praise any and all efforts.

   - *Not treating our children as individuals.* Recognize the uniqueness of each individual. Know your children and the things that make them feel loved and appreciated.

- *Nagging.* Reminding can be positive, but if not measured, can morph into nagging. Children cope with nagging by becoming selectively deaf to it.
- *Continual fault finding.* How many adults do you know who complained they never could please their dad? To not have this be part of what your child remembers 10, 20, 30 years from now, he or she has to believe you are their greatest fan.
- *Failure to appreciate their attempts to please and their simple kindnesses.* Our children really want to please us. Shoot for a 10 to 1 ratio, praise to correction. Every day.
- *Communicating that your child is interrupting your life.* Or your plans. Or your career. Continually communicate how important they are to you. Let them know your thoughts.

2. Name three from this list to focus on in the coming weeks.

Chapter 20

Fathers With Their Sons

Imagine you embark on a hike through the woods with two of your sons and your foot stumbles on something. You pick the item up and knock off the years of dirt. You do not recognize it, but on examination it appears to be some sort of tool. Obviously designed to do something, but what?

You hope the features will give clues to its purpose. What was this created to be? Your investigation is interrupted as a walnut hurls past your head. It was launched by one of your sons and intended for his brother on the other side of you. Another walnut whizzes past your head from the opposite side. Distracted with your pondering, you unwittingly stood in the midst of a walnut war.

Are you observing just another episode of chaos breaking out or are you observing a specific design in your sons? Their characteristics were created for a purpose. Even their delight in beaning their brother with a walnut is evidence of their design. The raw material in a young boy cannot be missed.

These qualities sometimes take the form of, or look like, bad behavior which needs correction, such as turning everything he touches into a weapon. But think of these behaviors as ones to be directed rather than corrected and consider how fathers take a vital role in this task.

During the various stages of a boy's development, these qualities will take on different looks, morph, and exchange places for the most dominant of the moment. It is critical for fathers to recognize and foster these qualities in their boys. What is the father's role in raising his boys to be men? What is the Creator's plan for you and your sons?

Moses tells us in Genesis that God created man and woman in his image. He commanded them to be fruitful and multiply and rule over the good, created world.

In *Future Men: Raising Boys to Fight Giants*, Douglas Wilson says, "Men are created to exercise dominion over the earth; they are fitted to be husbandmen, tilling the earth; they are equipped to be saviors, delivering from evil; they are expected to grow up into wisdom, becoming sages; and they are designed to reflect the image and glory of God."[1]

Dads, as you teach, train, and direct your son, consider these five aspects of manhood, according to Wilson:

1. *Lords.* Our boys always wanted to conquer the land, whether the back yard, the woods behind our house, or the family farm. Even when young, they evaluated every location for its potential for building an impregnable fort.

Boys should learn to be lords in the earth, adventurous, and visionary.

2. *Husbandmen.* In preparation for manhood, boys must learn to be hardworking. In their work, encourage them to be patient and careful.

3. *Saviors.* Boys must learn to be strong, sacrificial, courageous, and good.

4. *Sages.* Boys naturally want to "know stuff." They want to be smart and appear smart to others. Boys must learn to be thoughtful, teachable, and studious. Show them the masculinity of wisdom, books, and intellectual discussion. Sitting around the dinner table discussing important topics should be exciting. We want our boys to aspire to have something of value to share with others and wisdom to impart to their own sons and daughters.

5. *Glory-bearers.* Men should fulfill their responsibility to be representative, responsible, and holy. We must teach our boys to embrace this same responsibility.

Fathers in the home are to model these gifts and instruct their sons in them. Whether your son is four years old, fourteen or twenty-four, you see these qualities in them. Model appropriate expression and point them out to your son as being good.

Have faith!

Look at the present and see what it will become—through grace, good works, discipline, and training. Know your little boys are future men. God designed and gifted them in unique ways to one day fulfill their role and position of manhood.

Celebrate your son's desire to exercise dominion over the earth, build something, deliver from evil, gather new information, and reflect the image of God.

Consider and Apply:

1. How often have you heard, "Boys will be boys?" The truth is, we must *allow* and *encourage* boys to be boys. Do you recognize the five aspects of manhood in your son?
2. How can you find the balance between *correcting* and *directing* your son's behavior? Do you give him opportunities to display his gifts in appropriate ways?
3. Moms, name ways you can affirm God-given qualities in both your husband and your son.

Resources:

- Douglas Wilson, *Future Men: Raising Boys to Fight Giants* (Moscow, Idaho: Canon Press, 2001)

Chapter 21

Fathers With Their Daughters

Dads, have you ever thought of yourself as a superhero? You might as well design your signature cape now because, to your young daughter, you *are* a superhero. She sees you as not only smarter than anyone else, but the strongest person she knows.

In an interview with FamilyLife Today, Meg Meeker, M.D. spoke directly to fathers. "You are larger than life when we're little...Now, what are you going to do with that?"[1]

Meeker explains how our daughters want someone in authority, someone they respect who believes in them. It may seem enough to say, "I just want you to be happy." Or, to think the main thing your daughter needs is someone to believe in her dreams and chase after her, applauding and chanting, "Go, Girl, you can do it!"

This *is* important. However, if this is as deep as your interactions with her go, she is missing out on prime opportunities to receive your wisdom.

Indeed, your daughter relishes the times you cheer her on. When she turns and flashes that melt-your-heart smile as you run down the sidelines...well, it melts your heart. In addition to this, though, she needs you to help guide her to an understanding of her design and purpose.

Who is this person you both should believe in?

Your daughter has been given many gifts. Even if she is quite young, you already see them. These gifts are bestowed so she may be God's image bearer.

Do you often ask: "Who is this amazing young woman?"

Do you wonder: "Who can I be and what can I do to encourage her so she can find joy and be a blessing to others?"

Dads, you may be thinking this is a very tall order, but we can simplify it with a three-step process.

First, get to know the gifts God has given to your daughter. Note the similar traits of the women described in Proverbs 31:10-31, I Timothy 5:9-10, and Titus 2:3-5. When God completed the human race with the creation of woman, he gave her these characteristics for blessing and preserving mankind. All women have these gifts by design. This is true even if they do not know how to use them or even if the gifts are obscured or misdirected by sin.

Next, look for these qualities. How many of these gifts do you already see in your daughter?

- Faithfulness and a desire to bless others
- Wisdom
- Industry and creativity
- Desire to care for her household, working hard to make others comfortable and safe
- Kindness and generosity toward those in need

Finally, note these qualities when they surface and point them out to her. Be specific. These are qualities her husband and children will one day praise her for. You may see them in simple ways depending on your daughter's age—taking good care of her belongings, saving money for a gift for someone, helping with chores, reading to a sibling. The list will be long.

Follow "Way to go" with "I love how you showed kindness to that lady by holding the door for her," or "Thank you for being a good friend to your sister when she was sad." When she is older, you may say, "I am so proud of the way you stood your ground on what you believe and didn't sway with peer pressure. God will honor your faithfulness."

Regardless of your daughter's age—young, teen, or grown—this intentional way of communicating your appreciation for her God-given gifts will only strengthen your relationship. You will build her confidence as the young woman she was designed to be.

Consider and Apply:

1. How does God describe women in Proverbs 31:10-31, I Timothy 5:9-10, and Titus 2:3-5? What qualities (gifts) do you see in your daughter? How can you encourage your daughter by verbalizing what you observe in her?
2. Dr. Meg Meeker describes Dad as his daughter's first love, protector, and leader.[2] How do you see yourself in these roles? Where can you commit to improving your relationship with your daughter?

Resources:

- Meg Meeker, *Strong Fathers, Strong Daughters: 10 Secrets Every Father Should Know* (Regenery Publishing, 2015)
- Meg Meeker, *Raising a Strong Daughter in a Toxic Culture:11 Steps to Keep Her Happy, Healthy, and Safe* (Regenery Publishing, 2020)
- James Dobson, *Dads and Daughters* (Tyndale Momentum, 2014)

Passage VIII

Help Your Children
Discern God's Call

"...we exhorted each one of you and encouraged
you and charged you to walk in a manner worthy of
God who calls you into his own kingdom and
glory."
—I Thessalonians 2:12

For each of our children, the Christian life is a
life of responding to God's voice.

Through our instruction and encouragement,
we help our children to know and love God and to
heed the call into his kingdom.

Chapter 22

Let the Children Come

Our backyard pool is a long way from the Jordan River where Jesus himself was baptized by John the Baptist. But a few times in the past several years, up to one hundred fifty people stood around the pool.

They cheered and rejoiced as, one by one, individuals declared their faith in Jesus Christ and were baptized. The majority of those being baptized were children ranging in age from six-years-old to teens.

All of their testimonies were simple.

They had decided to follow Jesus and profess him to be their Savior, declaring their belief by a public baptism. With each one, we shared their excitement and responded by affirming their decision with applause and singing.

Often Christian parents and grandparents wonder what their role should be in guiding their children's decision to be baptized. We want to know what the children understand, to be sure they are "ready" and not just conforming to our desire for them.

It is also natural for us to require more from them than the simple faith they express--more understanding of sin, of the cross, and the nature of the forgiveness Christ purchased. Because of their youth, we sometimes hold them back and discount their simple desire to know and follow Jesus.

How much do they know? How much more do they need to understand before they can come to Christ?

To illustrate this point which often baffles parents, I (Stan) thought about an experience many years ago, on a road trip to California for business. The scenery was spectacular as my car approached a rugged mountainous area.

Darkness arrived with a sky full of stars, but no moon to illuminate my surroundings. My headlights revealed a long, massive bridge ahead. As I moved on to the bridge, I wondered what lurked beneath.

At the time, I only understood I needed to be on that bridge. Who made it or why it was made was not relevant at the time. On my return trip along the same route, the bridge appeared in bright daylight.

When the enormous, jagged and deep canyon became visible ahead, I marveled at the bridge's construction and fully understood its purpose. Able to see the awful chasm below, I crossed that bridge with a new appreciation which included a healthy dose of fear and thankfulness.

The account of Jesus receiving little children is a familiar story recorded for us in Matthew, Mark, and Luke. Imagine this scene...Word has traveled through the community that Jesus is there.

The townspeople rush to see him—young, old, parents with babies, the lame and the blind.

Many are needy and hope this man can heal them. Some seek words of encouragement, and some are merely curious. All have heard of the one who teaches and performs miracles, and they want to see him for themselves and receive a blessing.

In Luke 18:15-17, Luke tells how parents brought infants and young children to Jesus so he could receive and bless them. You might imagine the disciples would welcome the parents *and* their children as they displayed their faith.

However, the disciples rebuked the parents for bringing their children. Perhaps they thought Jesus did not have time for children or that his teaching was above these young people. Jesus was a busy man, after all.

Maybe they thought there was something more the children must do or understand before they could be received by the Son of God.

Seeing what took place, Jesus stopped the disciples from excluding the children. His instruction to the adults was clear. "Let the little children come to me, and do not hinder them, for to such belongs the kingdom of God."

Jesus welcomed the children into his arms and Mark 10:16 tells us he blessed them, laying his hands on them. Some of the children were quite young, brought to Jesus by their believing parents.

Others no doubt approached him on their own.

Luke records Jesus' words. "Truly, I say to you, whoever does not receive the kingdom of God like a child shall not enter it."

Notice Luke places this account between the story of the prayers of the Pharisee and the tax collector and the story of the rich young ruler.

The Pharisee approached Jesus with pride and arrogance in his piety. The rich young ruler came to Jesus with much material wealth, believing it would save him. The tax collector came to God with nothing to offer, nothing to claim--without wealth, pride, merit, or arrogance.

All are to come to Jesus with humility. Simply, humbly...as young children to be received into Jesus' arms.

The offer from Jesus has always been, and always will be, "Come!"

Consider and Apply:

1. Consider John Calvin's words. "If it is right that children would be brought to Christ, why should they not be admitted to baptism, the symbol of our communion and fellowship with Christ? If the kingdom of heaven is theirs, why should they be denied the sign by which access, as it were, is opened to the Church?"[1]
2. Read Acts 16:31-34 and Matthew 28:19-20. Baptism is an outward declaration of one's inclusion into the covenant community of Christ's followers. Why is it important? What is the instruction to parents?

Chapter 23

Receiving and Believing

Charles Spurgeon rightly declares, "The call of the Christian faith is the gentle word, 'Come.' From the first moment of your spiritual life until you are ushered into glory, the language of Christ to you will be, '*Come,* come unto me.'"[1]

Once your children have responded to the gentle call of Christ to come, how do they understand the idea of coming to God's kingdom and glory? The idea of being called into God's kingdom and glory is difficult for even parents to grasp.

The easiest way is to understand we are simply called into a place of learning. Jesus said, "Take my yoke upon you, and learn of me" (Matthew 11:29).

When the disciples were called into God's kingdom, they entered a grand adventure of observing and learning from Jesus. For the disciples, their time with him can be compared to walking through life with a friend. In this case, one who is an all-knowing teacher. Jesus introduced an invisible kingdom he said was already in their midst (Luke 17:21). How could they possibly understand it?

In his classic work, *The Training of the Twelve*, A.B. Bruce likens the disciples to children. "In the early period of their discipleship, hearing and seeing seem to have been the main occupation of the twelve. They were then like children born into a new world, whose first course of lessons consists in the use of their senses in observing the wonderful objects by which they are surrounded."[2]

Jesus not only taught them who God is and what he has done, but how the citizens should live. In his teaching on the Mount of Olives, Jesus describes the character and way of life that can only be lived by the supernatural help of God's Spirit (Matthew Chapters 5-7).

On one occasion, the disciples came to Jesus with the question of who would be the greatest in this kingdom. They proved they were still novices. Jesus used the question to teach them the virtue of humility. He called a child to himself to be the illustration for this important lesson.

Matthew records in Chapter 18:1-4, "At that time the disciples came to Jesus, saying, 'Who is the greatest in the kingdom of heaven?' And calling to him a child, he put him in the midst of them and said, 'Truly, I say to you, unless you turn and become like children, you will never enter the kingdom of heaven. Whoever humbles himself like this child is the greatest in the kingdom of heaven.'"

Jesus and the disciples walked nearly everywhere they went. Walking and talking. Their understanding was built gradually, one observation and lesson at a time. Writing of the disciples as they observed wonders and miracles, A.B. Bruce noted, "They enjoy anew the sensation of amazement."[3]

Christian parents formally invite their children to engage in a "life walk" of approximately eighteen or twenty years. As Jesus did with his disciples, we can capture every opportunity in daily life as a vehicle for instruction. Speaking about mankind in general, Paul in Romans 1:19 says, "For what can be known about God is plain to them, because God has shown it to them."

We could generate hundreds of topics to discuss with our children as we walk through life with them. Here are a few to consider:

- Jesus created all things.
- Jesus sustains all things.
- He plans for our fulfillment now and in the future.
- We are to live differently.
- We have a sure hope.
- He will be with us always.

Consider and Apply:

1. As you walk through life with your children, emphasize God's wonderful design and purpose in the created world. How are you leading them to the Creator? "Man was created to be a spectator of this formed world, and [his] eyes were given him, that he might by looking on so beautiful a picture, be led up to the Author himself"[4] (Calvin).

2. Discipleship occurs every day. Some have said it happens at under two miles per hour (walking speed). In other words, discipleship happens slowly over time. Are you making disciples at under two miles per hour? Identify at least three ways you can be more intentional in your training.

3. The best teachers anticipate questions and are prepared for instruction. Through shared discovery, they lead their disciples to greater understandings. How are you preparing to walk and talk through life with your family? What steps can you take to strengthen your ability to guide your children?

Chapter 24

Living in God's Kingdom

We never tire of stories of kings and their kingdoms, of good kings and bad and all the subjects they rule over. Our created story worlds are inhabited with heroes and villains as they traffic in truth, lies and intrigue.

Add some princesses, princes and dragons and we have the making of a great fable or fairytale or even a 4D video game. All guarantee the epic battles we love followed by the much-anticipated rescue.

Yet, we realize all these characters are present in our own world. We even have two warring kings and their kingdoms and a dragon, "the dragon, that ancient serpent" (Revelation 20:2).

But our world is not a stage for fables; it is the stage for eternity's greatest story, the story of the coming of Christ to affect our rescue, set us free, and fully restore us to God.

Jesus said this fallen world has a ruler who has "no claim on me" (John 14:30). Jesus came not only to establish his rule but to inaugurate an entirely new kingdom. Though they struggled to understand this unseen kingdom, the disciples slowly realized Jesus brought different teaching to create a new way of living.

Since this unseen world is apprehended by faith, the rulers and religious leaders could not understand it (John 3:1-21). At his trial, Pilate asked Jesus if he was King of the Jews. Jesus answered, "My kingdom is not of this world. If my kingdom were of this world, my servants would have been fighting, that I might not be delivered over to the Jews. But my kingdom is not from the world" (John 18:36).

Thus, the dilemma. We live in a physical world but, as believers in Jesus Christ, we are citizens of God's unseen kingdom as well.

Even though this dual citizenship may be a difficult concept to grasp, we understand as Christ followers and kingdom citizens we are to live differently in our physical world. Though all inhabitants share the same blessings, Christians living according to God's kingdom enjoy these blessings with thanksgiving. "For everything created by God is good, and nothing is to be rejected if it is received with thanksgiving" (I Timothy 4:4).

Several terms are used in the Christian world to describe this dual citizenship, including the temporal and the eternal kingdoms, the earthly and the heavenly kingdoms. Many theologians call this understanding the already and the not-yet of Christ's kingdom.

We *already* possess it by faith, and we live accordingly even though Christ's kingdom has *not yet* been fully established.

R.C. Sproul clearly explains the task of the church in making the kingdom of God manifest to the world. "John Calvin said it is the task of the church to make the invisible kingdom visible. We do this by living in such a way that we bear witness to the reality of the kingship of Christ in our jobs, our families, our schools, and even our checkbooks, because God in Christ is King over every one of these spheres of life. The only way the kingdom of God is going to be manifest in this world before Christ comes is if we manifest it by the way we live as citizens of heaven and subjects of the King."[1]

When our boys were teens, we sometimes stopped them at the front door as they left the house. We might give them a hug or touch their arm and say, "Remember who you are." They heard, "Remember you have dual citizenship." This message is not just for teenagers but for those who live in anticipation of God's future kingdom. What we believe about God will determine not only how we conduct ourselves in this world but where our future hope lies.

Consider and Apply:

1. How do Christians live *in* the world according to Christ's kingdom but not be *of* the world?
2. How will you use this understanding to help your children enjoy the good world God created?
3. The historical Christian confession is, "Jesus is Lord." It is also true if Christ is not the Lord *of* all, he is not the Lord *at* all. In what ways are you demonstrating Christ's lordship?

Passage IX

Teach for the Worthy Walk

"…we exhorted each one of you and encouraged you and charged you to walk in a manner worthy of God, who calls you into his own kingdom and glory."
—I Thessalonians 2:12

What joy could be greater than seeing our children walk with God?

This is the goal of all that we do, and all that God is doing through us.

Chapter 25

You've Been Charged!

In my corporate life, I (Stan) attended many staff meetings led by our well-respected chief executive. Since he was the boss, he had authority and thus the right to impose obligations on the rest of us.

Before his corporate position, he served in an honored branch of the military and led many men into combat. Our corporate world was not exactly combat but, when he looked at me and gave me an assignment, I listened attentively. You might say I snapped to attention.

When our meeting ended, there was no doubt I had been *charged* with a task. I knew the charge was not merely to dabble or give some lesser effort to the task but to see it through. Every assignment had a deadline and, on the way back to my office, I worked on a plan to get started.

I loved hearing, "Well done." I also would have hated to say, "Sir, I haven't gotten around to it yet...Sir."

He had charged me with an assignment and his desire quickly became my desire. I wanted to please him and prove his trust in me.

In this routine scenario, three questions were answered:

- *Who is charging me?*
- *What is he charging me to do?*
- *What should my response be?*

Was fear part of my motivation? It was, but what kind of fear? Christians have often been confused by the idea of being motivated by a fear of God. The Bible uses the word "fear" at least 300 times in reference to God.

Martin Luther explored the meaning of fearing God and made a distinction between what he called filial fear and servile fear. R.C. Sproul further explained Luther's work.[1] Servile fear is the type of fear one might have in anticipation of physical punishment by an authority.

In contrast to servile fear, filial fear is drawn from the Latin concept of family. Consider the child who has respect and love for his parents and who wants to please them. The child may fear offending those he loves, not because he is afraid of punishment, but because he is afraid of disrupting the source of love and security. The goal of the father/child relationship is to draw us to God rather than away. An understanding of filial fear leads us to honor and obedience.

Romans 8:15 says, "For you did not receive the spirit of slavery to fall back into fear, but you have received the Spirit of adoption as sons, by whom we cry, 'Abba! Father!'"

Now consider what Paul is charging his spiritual children to do. He is charging them to walk in a way consistent with their new identity as Christians. They are to have the characteristics of their Father and also their spiritual parent, Paul.

The charge to parents is to possess an identity from Christ so they can say to their children, "be imitators of me, as I am of Christ" (1 Corinthians 11:1). We cannot pass on a faith we do not ourselves possess. We cannot be casual or even neutral toward faith.

If our children are inclined to imitate us, we want to be worthy of being imitated.

Consider and Apply:

1. Read Proverbs 1:7 and Proverbs 14:2. Considering your understanding of filial fear, restate these verses in your own words.
2. Read I Kings 2:1-4. How does the charge to Solomon compare to Paul's charge to his followers?

Chapter 26

Table Talk

One of our favorite publications is *Tabletalk*, a monthly journal of articles and devotions published by R.C. Sproul's ministry, Ligonier.[1] Dr. Sproul adopted the title from a series of notes taken from Martin Luther's table discussions with his students and other visitors.

This type of table conversation was also the preferred method of discussing truth and its application for Francis and Edith Schaeffer. The Schaeffers established a retreat in Switzerland which they called "L'Bri," French for "shelter."

People came from all over the world to engage with the Schaeffers. They gathered around the dinner table and explored the truths of Christianity together.

We have the wonderful privilege of living literally around the corner from several of our grandchildren. The four oldest are teen boys and their ages worked perfectly for our first attempt at hosting our own version of discussions we call Table Talk.

The boys seemed excited to come over and discuss topics on their teenage minds. Our offer of chili and ice cream closed the deal.

A conversation about identity was on our minds and is a big topic for kids this age. How does identity create expectation? How does expectation drive behavior? We had the perfect opener.

A few days before our first meeting, we came across an article in a hometown newspaper. It contained some big news, though not unexpected. An Oklahoma high school wrestling team had just won their third straight and 43rd State Championship, a national record.

The boys viewed the headlines and discussed how they thought this remarkable record could have been accomplished by a small, rural community. One suggested the obvious--the athletes were farm boys who grew up wrestling cattle and hay bales.

The youngest wondered if it was the uniform. He offered his answer with a grin, hoping to get a laugh, but we later came back to his answer and found it stimulated some rich discussion.

We finally landed on the important ingredient of "expectation." The history and the tradition created by a long line of individual wrestling records created a continual expectation of excellence.

We also noted expectations do not always line up with just athletic performance but, more importantly, with character performance. We discussed this in light of our own family, touching on the meaning of tradition, accountability, legacy, reputation, and yes, what it means to "put on the uniform."

Our first Table Talk was lively and provocative and, from what we observed, meaningful for the boys. We could tell they liked being able to join in on big ideas and explore significant concepts.

All of the boys left our home looking forward to the next time we could meet. Why did this work? Why were the boys ready to engage in real topics?

- We created an opportunity for conversation in a non-threatening environment. This was our time together. We offered them a safe place where they could feast on some solid food and ideas.

- We brought a good question we knew would inspire them toward big ideas. Then we let them talk. Our minds are often lazy. Most conversation, unless prompted by a question, tends to flow to the easy and familiar.

- We worked to solve a story problem together. This is how Jesus taught his disciples and this is how we teach our young disciples, utilizing the skills we have acquired to further explain the truth.

In anticipating more Table Talks with the four teens, as well as preparing for our remaining nine grandchildren in the future, we designated a file folder for collecting ideas and questions.

What is worldview? How does our worldview inform our behavior? What is peer pressure and how can we stand up to it? What is the meaning of masculinity? Of femininity?

Parents, though this idea may need some adjustment for your family, you can start your own Table Talk tradition. Different from "family meetings." Different from "Sit down, your parents want to talk to you."

Make sure they feel this is their time. When your teen says, "Hey, when can we do Table Talk again?" you will know you are on to something significant.

Consider and Apply:

1. Describe how your family might benefit from your own version of Table Talk. How would you implement this time together?
2. Ask your teen to invite a couple friends over for a meal and Table Talk. Be prepared with some good questions for discussion. Be flexible and be patient. Let them talk. Enjoy the moments and have fun!
3. Keep a folder of interesting topics for future Table Talks. Ask your teen to add their ideas to the folder.

Chapter 27

Realistic Expectations

We will never forget the days of lining up four little boys on the couch for pep talks. Expectations had been explained and discussed. The boys had received instruction and the desired behavior had been modeled. Now we were ready to try it in the field. We were going to the store!

All of us. At the same time.

Imagine a little league team piling hands in the middle of the circle—*Yes! We can do this!* We were all in.

Well, we would love to say Field Work always went well. Granted, sometimes it did, and we celebrated our success big time. Sometimes, our little troops displayed an obvious need for more practice.

The time one boy vanished and was discovered peering and waving at us from inside the upright freezer case amongst the TV dinners. Or the time a boy (yes, the same boy) disappeared and, just as we were getting frantic and ready to barricade the exit doors, he popped up from the center of a clothing rounder.

Okay, we admit *now* it is funny. At the time, our job was to understand training is a *process*, adjust instruction, and try again. Without angry words, without scolding, and without despair, we were to remain calm and keep on training.

This is not always easy to do.

Rachel Jankovic is a mom of five children. In her book, *Loving the Little Years: Motherhood in the Trenches,* she says the following about children:

"It is very easy for us to forget about the progress they make and to ignore the problems that they no longer wrestle with. If you have been faithfully disciplining your children, I guarantee you there are many, many problems that they no longer struggle with...Try to notice these little mile markers on the path of sanctification. If the sins have changed, it can be a sign of growth.

It is not as though our children are going to emerge from their current problems into perfect holiness, if only we give them enough swats. They are going to emerge from one set of problems into the next, and that is good. That is the way of the Christian walk. Treat sins that your children struggle with like basic math. Practice, practice, and you'll get it!"[1]

As difficult as it is for parents to give up perfectionist thinking, we have to look at everything as a training opportunity. Parenting is training and training is a *process*, not an event.

It always aims at something (the end goal) and always involves the following:

1) Instruction

2) Modeling
3) Praise or Reward
4) Consequence
5) Repetition
6) Field Work
7) Advancement

If we lined up a few hundred parents and had them indicate which one of these is the most wearisome, Step 5 would win hands down.

How many times have I told you...? Didn't we go over this yesterday? I can't believe I'm having to tell you this again!

How wonderful it would be if we only had to tell our young charges something once! As the saying goes, *don't hold your breath*. This rarely happened in our home. What we observe in our young trainees is the product of our training process; the good and the bad. If we get to Field Work and "my kids just don't seem to be getting it," then as trainers, we repeat the process from the beginning. If we do not get the behavior we want to see, we adjust the instruction. The responsibility is on the trainer.

According to a 2009 study published in the European Journal of Social Psychology, it takes 18 to 254 days for a person to form a new habit. The study also concluded that, on average, it takes 66 correct completions of a task for a new behavior to become automatic.

There is no one-size-fits-all figure, which is why this time frame is so broad; some habits are easier to form than others, and some people may find it easier than others to develop new behaviors. In addition, the researchers found missing an opportunity here and there to perform the new behavior did not affect the overall habit formation process.[2]

Manage your expectations and give yourself and your children some grace. Brushing teeth properly, turning those dirty socks right side out, speaking kindly to a sibling…Depending on the task and the person, the new behavior may be formed in a mere few days. But most will take much longer.

What does this mean for your children? Every child has a unique personality. Some will develop good habits or change bad habits easier than others. Your task as parents is to train wisely…some kids are more compliant; some are more strong-willed. What does this mean for you?

It means *be realistic*!

It takes time to form good habits of behavior. For our children's sake (and our own) we have to see parenting as a process. Help your child have success and do not lose heart. It will get better. If Field Work fails, regroup, reteach, and try it again!

Consider and Apply:

1. Read II Peter 1:12-13, II Peter 3:1, Philippians 3:1, Romans 15:14-15. Peter and Paul did not just tell their spiritual children something once. Since their desires were for them to grow in maturity and faith, they were patient in reminding the people of things that are true.

2. As Rachel Jankovic encouraged us, how can we notice—and celebrate—the little mile markers on the path to our child's sanctification? Remind yourselves daily of the progress they have made. Give clear and specific affirmation to your children regarding the growth you observe.

Resources:

Rachel Jankovic, *Loving the Little Years: Motherhood in the Trenches* (Moscow, Idaho: Canon Press, 2010)

Passage X

Pray Without Ceasing

"And we also thank God constantly for this, that when you received the Word of God, which you heard from us, you accepted it not as the word of men but as what it really is, the Word of God, which is at work in you believers."

—I Thessalonians 2:13

Oh, for our children to hear us rejoicing over them for the work of God in their lives!

Our prayers are the means of calling down blessings for our children and the means of giving us the confidence that God can be believed.

Prayer produces courage and patience in both us and our children.

Chapter 28

Why Pray?

If we believe God is sovereign and orders the world, why pray? God is all-knowing, all-powerful, and omnipotent. "Who has measured the Spirit of the Lord, or what man shows him his counsel?" (Isaiah 40:13).

Note the psalmist's words: "Whatever the Lord pleases, he does, in heaven and on earth, in the seas and all deeps" (Psalm 135:6). See also Psalm 115:3. "Our God is in the heavens; he does all that he pleases."

Do our prayers really affect *anything?* In our exploration here, you will see the following: God uses our prayers, Christians have a ministry of intercession, and through praying, we are also changed.

When Paul and his ministry partners wrote I Thessalonians 2:13, "We thank God constantly…," we understand they were thankful for the fruit they saw in the lives of the church members. This fruit was the result of God's gracious response to their continual prayers. By his thanksgiving, Paul acknowledged God as the source of the growth they observed.

From other letters Paul wrote, we learn his love for the people prompted him to a continual ministry of prayer. He always asked God for protection for the churches and for their spiritual growth.

He often prayed their understanding would increase as they came to know the one who was now their father. Paul's prayers were intercessory, like the pleadings of Christ for his church.

Throughout scripture we see God *delights* to honor the intercessions of his own children on behalf of others (Proverbs 15:8, NASB). Knowing this, parents can be confident they have received a great invitation to pray for their children!

Though we see God's responses connected to Paul's pleadings, we wonder about our own sometimes inconsistent prayers. Do they also change things? Even our children? We hope the answer is, "Yes!"

As we reason through these questions, we know the most God-like attribute of God is his sovereignty. The Bible teaches us that our sovereign God is also fatherly in his affection toward his children.

With his fatherly nature, he condescends to use prayer, even our prayers, as the means to bring about his purposes. Though this wonderful truth may be hard to understand and may not answer all of our questions, it answers the most important question, "Why pray?"

God delights to use our prayers. This is why we pray in faith. This is the great promise to believers and the great encouragement to believing parents.

Not only does God use our believing prayers to accomplish his will, but he also uses our prayers to *change us*. A great benefit is offered to us in that prayer and praise promote the growth of the spiritual life.

In prayer and praise our burdens are removed, our faith is increased, and our hope is excited. This is why God commands us to come to him with all our requests.

The promise from the Bible is, "Ask and it will be given to you" (Matt 7:7). Doesn't it seem strange when we attempt to gather our own resources rather than embrace what God has so liberally offered to us?

You can see that as we pray, our eyes are no longer focused on our own efforts to meet needs, but they are turned to God and his provision. Our dependence deepens as we anticipate his blessing. By praying, we are preparing ourselves to receive these benefits with thanksgiving and, therefore, God receives the glory.

We know God is the sovereign dispenser of all good and invites us to present our requests to him. Parents, let us not allow these great treasures to remain buried in the ground[1] (Calvin, paraphrased).

Consider and Apply:

1. Read Luke 6:12 and Luke 11:1-4. Jesus was God-incarnate, sinless, spotless, and perfect. Yet, Jesus prayed. Describe what these verses tell us about the importance of prayer. How should we approach God in prayer?

2. "If all these things are to be had by merely knocking at mercy's door, O my soul, knock hard this morning, and ask large things of thy generous Lord. Leave not the throne of grace till all thy wants have been spread before the Lord, and until by faith thou hast a comfortable prospect that they shall be all supplied…No unbelief should hinder when Jesus promises"[2] (Spurgeon). What "large things" are you asking of your generous Lord for your children? List obstacles that hinder you from being active in prayer.

3. "Hence all the passages throughout Scripture in which we are commanded to pray, are set up before our eyes as so many banners, to inspire us with confidence"[3] (Calvin). Consider keeping a prayer journal where you record specific prayers and recent answers. Use the journal to stay focused in prayer and gain confidence in God as answered prayers are revealed.

Chapter 29

Gaining Confidence in Prayer

Knowing the importance of prayer, parents want their prayers to have the desired effect, to be effectual, as theologians would say. Even with many verses to promote our confidence, in our own experience, prayer and confidence do not always go together.

We have all experienced what seems to be unanswered and unfruitful prayers and are often unsure we are asking for the right things.

However, we do know how to shop online. When the doorbell rings and a package appears on our porch, are we surprised? Do we exclaim in disbelief, "What is this? I wonder where it came from?"

Of course not! We were expecting the package because we had requested it. We believed it would eventually arrive. Can our prayers be like this? Can we move from surprise to expectation and confidence?

Who may come to a holy God and make a request? The Bible tells us in Hebrews 11:6, "And without faith it is impossible to please him, for whoever would draw near to God must believe that he exists and that he rewards those who seek him."

Paul wrote to the Galatian church "for in Christ Jesus you are all sons of God, through faith" (Galatians 3:26). This is the good news we need! Even though none of us is worthy to come forward in our own name, we now have access to God through our own advocate and mediator, Jesus Christ. John Calvin says this is the key by which believers open the door of prayer.[1] What an invitation we have, as his children! We may now come to God as our Father for he sees us in his Son.

He is pleased with us, and ready to hear our request and provide what we seek. In summary, we pray to our Father by the merits of his Son with the enabling of the Holy Spirit. Even though much can be taught of how the third person of the Trinity helps us pray, perhaps the most important is he assures us of our relationship to God the Father. This is important because with the awareness of sin in our lives, we feel unworthy to approach God with the familial confidence we may desire.

Even with access granted to us to come to God as our Father, and with assurance and help from the Holy Spirit, we want to ask for the right things. "And this is the confidence that we have toward him, that if we ask anything according to his will, he hears us. And if we know that he hears us in whatever we ask, we know that we have the requests that we have asked of him" (1 John 5:14-15).

If we want to pray expectantly for what God desires (according to his will), we could not do better than to follow Paul's example as he prayed for the Thessalonians. We are glad Paul's requests for the Thessalonians are not vague as he prayed that they would:

- Imitate Paul and the Lord (1:6).
- Walk in a manner worthy of God, who calls them into his kingdom and glory (2:12).
- Receive the Word of God and accept it and it would work in their lives (2:13).
- Abstain from sexual immorality and know how to control their own bodies in holiness and honor (4:3).
- Not transgress and wrong their fellow Christians (4:6).

In addition, Paul prayed he would be able to supply what is lacking in their faith (3:10). Consider what Jesus taught his disciples about praying persistently, recorded for us in Luke's gospel.

In Luke Chapter 11 Jesus tells a parable about a man who is unwilling to provide his neighbor with three loaves of bread. It is late, and the neighbor does not want to be bothered, but the man is persistent, and the neighbor finally relents.

He gets up and provides the loaves, not because he was a friend, but because the man was persistent. Jesus concludes with these words in verses 9 and 10. "And I tell you, ask, and it will be given to you; seek, and you will find; knock, and it will be opened to you. For everyone who asks receives, and the one who seeks finds, and to the one who knocks it will be opened."

We will let John Calvin give us our final encouragement to be "animated to pray with the sure hope of succeeding."[2]

Consider and Apply:

1. Our good intentions often run afoul of our time commitments. Will you set aside time to pray for your children?
2. Will you pray for your own needs as parents and ask others to pray for you, as well?
3. When we pray, remember "we are to ask only in so far as God permits."[3] However, we are encouraged to ask all that God offers. See I John 5:14.

Chapter 30

Rejoice Over Them!

When the Apostle Paul proclaims in I Thessalonians 2:13 that he is thanking God, he is also rejoicing. He rejoices as he sees the fruit of the labor described in previous verses. What an example for parents to follow!

Wouldn't it be wonderful if our children heard their parents give thanks to God for the specific work he is doing in their lives? It would be hard for a child to be discouraged or disgruntled or even disbelieving living in a house filled with this kind of rejoicing. Our children would flourish in such a home.

Instilling Motivation

Can you recall the people who encouraged you most during your formative years? Did their words motivate you to excel still more? Possibly they looked beyond your flaws of the moment and saw who you were becoming.

They saw things in you which you did not even see in yourself, and you wanted to prove they were right. This is a powerful motivation; to fulfill the potential someone sees in you. I (Stan) recall an experience from nearly fifty years ago which proves this point.

When I was in college, I had a difficult class in the Animal Science Department. We had taken a challenging test, our first test under a notorious professor. On the day he was to hand back our graded tests, everyone in the class broke into a sweat, including me.

The professor held up a test and announced, with a degree of surprise (and perhaps irritation), someone in the class made a perfect score. We all looked around assuming it was one of the usual brainy suspects. Well, I was shocked, along with everyone else, when he walked over and laid the test on my desk.

Wow, what happened? He just declared, in front of the entire class--I was a scholar. This was a transformative moment for me. I was determined to prove his declaration of my academic talent was not misplaced. Nor was it a fluke! It is no mystery I expended more effort in his class than any other class the rest of the semester.

Paul understood this truth as he wrote to churches. He often pointed out the evidence he saw demonstrating God's work in their lives. He set before them a vision of who God was conforming them to be. Consider the specific benefits for your own children as you thank God aloud for the growth you observe in them. As you do this, your children will:

- Connect what you see in them with the reality God is at work in their lives.
- Understand God is the source.
- Desire to grow more.
- Anticipate God's blessing.

Learning Doctrine and the Power of Prayer

What else happens when our children hear us pray? We teach them truth and even doctrine as we demonstrate prayer is serious work and a grand privilege.

Parents have a wonderful opportunity to model prayer, to teach their children how one should approach God in prayer, what to be thankful for, and what to request. Imagine how encouraged your children will be to hear you rejoice over them. Mention them by name as you go before God, calling out specific growth in character and wise decisions they have made.

Consider and Apply:

1. Read Luke 11:1. The disciples were impressed as they heard Jesus pray and they asked for instruction. Do you pray in such a way your children desire to imitate you?
2. Consider teaching your children doctrine as you pray aloud. What will you teach your children about God as you pray with them and over them?
3. How will your words spoken in prayer motivate your children to anticipate the person they are becoming? Pray intentionally for each child.

Passage XI

Demonstrate How God's Word Works

"And we also thank God constantly for this, that when you received the Word of God, which you heard from us, you accepted it not as the word of men but as what it really is, the Word of God, which is at work in you believers."

—I Thessalonians 2:13

As we are careful to instruct our children in the Word of God, we are also to model the life contained in this instruction.

The fruit will come when our children receive the Word, the Word they hear from us, and it will work in their lives because they believe it.

Chapter 31

Nurturing a Desire for Instruction

My kids don't listen to me! If they would just listen and obey, their lives (and ours) would be so much better. They always prefer to learn the hard way!

This is not just the cry of many parents; it was even the anguished cry of God concerning his own children in Deuteronomy 5:29. "Oh that they had such a heart as this always, to fear me and to keep all my commandments, that it might go well with them and with their descendants forever!"

In every era, parents want their children to honor and obey them for their good. This is one of God's top ten commands. Though some children want to please their parents, most simply want what they want.

To accomplish this, they are often willing to turn to any counselor who offers advice on how to accomplish their goal. Paul tells us that men seek out counselors according to their desires.

"For the time is coming when people will not endure sound teaching but having itching ears, they will accumulate for themselves teachers to suit their own passions…" (II Timothy 4:3).

Here is the challenge for parents. In a world continually offering your children instruction on how to get what they desire, will they listen to wisdom from a God they cannot see or hear?

For about eighteen years your children will be planted in your household where you will be the greatest source of God's wisdom, communicated by your lives and by your words. As the diligent farmer prepares the soil, Christian parenting is preparing children to receive God's words. Your preparation will include connecting their wants with your instruction and parental wisdom.

So, how to do this?

Remember how eager young children are when they ask you to read a story to them? You may have heard a chorus of, "Please, please read just one more!" Their plan may be to avoid going to bed, but often there is something more.

Children love to hear their parents read and they also desire to become readers themselves. With this motivation, children are easy to instruct. Why? Because they see your instruction as the way to get what they want.

Fast forward a few years when your children want to learn to catch or throw or hit the ball with the bat. "Come on Mom. Come on Dad, throw me one more pitch!" A few more years flash by and they are eager for you to teach them how to drive. The car promises a new freedom and they are ready to learn.

Don't overlook these seemingly small teaching opportunities. All of them prepare your children for the instruction you will provide in the more critical areas of life. If you have spent time instructing them in the life skills they *want*, you will have both the relationship and the opportunity to share with them valuable wisdom they *need*. Much like the diligent farmer, you have prepared good soil for God's Word to be received and produce fruit.

Consider and Apply:

1. Who are the sources your children value and seek out for information and instruction?
2. How do you prove your reliability and become the most valued source of information your children desire?

Chapter 32

How the Word Works

Costumes can be magical. Put a puppy dog costume on a small child and he may immediately drop to all fours and begin barking and whimpering. Put a long fancy princess dress on a little girl and she will begin walking like royalty--and twirling.

Children know how to "put on" a new identity and then immediately begin to act accordingly. You might say they have transformed. How many times have you observed your children at play like this?

They may identify with their new character until you finally convince them to remove the costume and get ready for bed.

In I Thessalonians 2:13, Paul is not describing mere child's play. We have come to perhaps the most important verse in this entire section of Paul's letter as it contains the wonderful promise of transformation.

Here Paul gives thanks for what every Christian parent desires for their children, that God's Word would be at work in them. This is what we want for ourselves, and this is certainly where our parenting is aimed.

How does the Word work in us and in our children? We know God's eternal plan is to conform Christians to the likeness of his Son. Consider Romans 8:29, "For those whom he (God) foreknew he also predestined to be conformed to the image of his Son, in order that he might be the firstborn among many brothers."

Thus, the work we observe will be in accordance with God's plan.

For God's Word to work, it must first be heard. "When you received the word of God, which you heard from us..." (I Thessalonians 2:13). How wonderful God chooses to use not only the printed Scriptures but human voices to communicate his most divine and powerful agent of transformation.

We must take care to communicate not just our own words but God's message. The Bible is the only source whereby we come to know who God is and understand who we are.

Through the process Paul describes, we actually *are* being renewed and transformed into a new image as we believe. Notice how Paul instructs the church in Ephesus in this process of putting off their former manner of life by putting on a new identity.

His instruction begins with teaching (the "hearing" and "receiving" of our current verse). He encourages the Ephesians "to put off your old self, which belongs to your former manner of life and is corrupt through deceitful desires, and to be renewed in the spirit of your minds, and to put on the new self, created after the likeness of God in true righteousness and holiness" (Ephesians 4:22-24).

His encouragement to the church in Colossae is the same. In this letter, Paul likens understanding this new identity to putting on a new garment after first removing the old one. "But now you must put them all away: anger, wrath, malice, slander, and obscene talk from your mouth. Do not lie to one another, seeing that you have put off the old self with its practices and have put on the new self, which is being renewed in knowledge after the image of its creator" (Colossians 3:8-10).

The result is our old habits and identity are replaced by our new habits and a new identity. This can occur dramatically and rapidly, and it can also occur more slowly over time. Both are evidence of the reality of God's Word working in us.

This is the process the Bible calls sanctification. Our sanctification will progress until we lay our body aside and are with Christ. Growth in Christ will be a continual series of this putting off and putting on which Paul describes. It is encouraging to know the Holy Spirit is given to us to instruct and aid us in this change, no matter how often it is repeated.

Consider and Apply:

1. Read Colossians 3:5-10. In what ways have you put off the old and put on the new? Is the transformation evident to your spouse, your children, and others around you? Remember this is not a "one and done" activity but a continual process of recognizing who we were and putting on who we are.
2. For the Word of God to work in our lives and the lives of our children, it must be heard. Do you regularly pray for God to grant hearing to you and your children?

Chapter 33

The Spirit at Work

Here on the prairie, the wind reveals itself most days. We even sing about the "waving wheat" and on some occasions, we watch the neighbor's trampoline tumble down the street. Though we could work to make the lyrics rhyme, the trampoline has not yet been immortalized in song.

In every case, we do not actually see the wind. We only observe its effects.

In his conversation with a Rabbi, Jesus used the wind to illustrate the Spirit's unseen work in the new birth. "The wind blows where it wishes, and you hear its sound, but you do not know where it comes from or where it goes. So it is with everyone who is born of the Spirit" (John 3:8).

In the same way Paul could not see the Holy Spirit, yet he observed the positive effects of the Spirit's work in the lives of the Thessalonians. We desire to see the effects in our own children, as well.

To understand the Holy Spirit's work, parents must first understand who he is. Theologians and councils have long understood God is one essence in three distinct persons (Westminster Confession of Faith).[1]

The nature and the working of our triune God could be understood in this way: the Father purposed our salvation, the Son purchased our salvation, and the Spirit, sent by the Father and the Son, applies the benefits of our salvation.

The Holy Spirit is a person as emphasized by Jesus in John 16. Eleven times, Jesus describes the Spirit using the pronouns he, him, and his.

Perhaps the most encouraging way for us to understand the Holy Spirit is to realize he possesses every attribute of Jesus, yet without a physical body. Think how important this understanding would be to the disciples as Jesus explains he will no longer be physically present with them. He assures them a helper will come.

"But because I have said these things to you, sorrow has filled your heart. Nevertheless, I tell you the truth: it is to your advantage that I go away, for if I do not go away, the Helper will not come to you. But if I go, I will send him to you" (John 16:6-7).

Now, imagine Jesus helping us, as he promised, even being with us in all of his ability and wisdom.

Jesus continues to tell the disciples of the Spirit's important work in revealing truth to their minds, the work we desire for our children and for ourselves. "When the Spirit of truth comes, he will guide you into all the truth, for he will not speak on his own authority, but whatever he hears he will speak, and he will declare to you the things that are to come. He will glorify me, for he will take what is mine and declare it to you. All that the Father has is mine; therefore, I said he will take what is mine and declare it to you" (John 16:13-15).

In his thorough book on the Holy Spirit, Sinclair Ferguson writes, "The coming of the Spirit is the equivalent of the indwelling of Jesus. This is for his disciples' good, since it implies such a close union with Christ that he dwells *in* them not merely *with* them."[2]

What is our part in this great work? Our task is to bring the truth of the gospel to our children. We provide this through studying the Bible with them and through our own words. Thankfully, the Spirit has the power to use our words, exhortations, and illustrations to effect change in us and our children.

In addition, we are to pray for the Spirit's work in their lives and to ask God to provide the help we need. "Nothing pleases our Lord better than to see his promises put in circulation; he loves to see his children bring them up to him, and say, 'Lord, do as you have said.' We glorify God when we plead his promises"[3] (Spurgeon).

Consider and Apply:

1. What challenges have you faced in explaining the triune God to your children?
2. In his *Institutes*, John Calvin gives a helpful summary of the work of the Holy Spirit. "…He is the *internal* teacher, by whose agency the promise of salvation, which would otherwise only strike the air or our ears, penetrates into our minds."[4] When we feel like our children are not listening to us at all, it is comforting to know the Holy Spirit, the internal teacher, can cause truth to penetrate their minds! Look for the effects of his working and tell your children the positive changes you see in them.

Passage XII

Be the One Your Children Want to Imitate

"For you, brothers, became imitators of the churches of God in Christ Jesus that are in Judea."
--I Thessalonians 2:14

Throughout their lives, our children will imitate someone.

They will usually imitate people whose character or actions they admire.

If we are careful to set before them a joyful character and noble vocation worthy to be imitated, they will imitate us as we follow Christ.

Chapter 34

What Are You Training Them to Hunt?

For an upland bird hunter, nothing is prettier than the sight of a young bird dog, especially one you have trained, locked up on point and holding steady. Is he pointing a nice covey? A single? Or a rooster pheasant trying to make himself invisible? It could be just a meadowlark or an armadillo rooting around. But you approach the weed patch confident he is pointing what you have trained him to hunt.

Bird dog puppies, no matter how good their parentage, do not naturally prefer to hunt pheasant and quail. They are only born with really good noses. And the world outside at puppy level is filled with fascinating scents.

Along with their natural ability, they have the curiosity to find out where those scents are coming from. In a world of bird scents, and everything else scents, they will find the same thrill in using their nose to locate meadowlarks and armadillos, skunks and porcupines.

In addition to learning the basic obedience commands, the goal of training a bird dog puppy is to teach it what the two of you will be hunting *together*.

Puppies will learn to hunt what we, their leaders, the big alpha dogs, are excited about; what we make a big deal over and praise them for. The concept is simple. They will hunt what we have pursued together.

They hunt because of relationship.

In time, they learn and will not give a meadowlark a sniff or be distracted when a big jackrabbit breaks from cover. As they continue to hunt, they even learn to think like a pheasant or a quail. Many times, I have watched an experienced English Setter cover several acres, most of it at full speed. He was very efficient and only went to the places with good cover for quail because he had learned from experience where the birds would most likely be.

Likewise, our children are born with a keen desire to explore their world. They will be attracted to whatever sparkles and shines, sometimes with terrible consequences as in a bird dog's encounter with a porcupine.

Through your relationship with them, they will learn to avoid what is dangerous. They will be excited to pursue *with you* the quarry *you* are hunting. Let it be the wisdom and understanding that Solomon urges.

"My son, if you receive my words and treasure up my commandments with you, making your ear attentive to wisdom and inclining your heart to understanding; yes, if you call out for insight and raise your voice for understanding, if you see it like silver and search for it as for hidden treasures, then you will understand the fear of the Lord and find the knowledge of God" (Proverbs 2:1-5).

Consider and Apply:

1. How would your children describe what is important to you? Reflect on recent conversations and consider what you are leading them to pursue.
2. Parents, be willing to be used by God in the lives of people who are placed in your path. And, if it happens when your children are with you to observe the interactions, the experience will enable them to see the gospel and the love of God in action. Include your children as you minister to others. Let them clearly see what you pursue.
3. Do you make wisdom attractive to your child? Scripture only describes two groups we can follow, the wise and the foolish. One should look attractive and the other something to avoid.

Chapter 35

Surviving the Teen Years

Several years ago, we were asked to speak to a home fellowship group about raising boys. They wanted to know, "How did your boys survive the teen years intact?" For us, that translated to "What were the factors that helped our sons manage the often confusing, temptation-ridden, troubling teenage years and enable them to come out on the other side in one piece, still walking with God?"

Hmmm—other than the grace of God, how *did* that happen?

Our sons were all in their 20s and 30s at the time, married, and some had children. The teen years seemed a long time ago. The upcoming talk caused us to spend some time reflecting on those years and how we *all* managed them.

Over the following week, we embarked on an informal research project by scheduling a time to talk to each of our boys. We asked them all the same simple question: *How did you make it through the teen years?*

They did not have an opportunity to talk to their brothers—only to give an answer based on their own experience. Each one of our sons, independent of the others, summarized their comments with a statement similar to this: "I was accountable to other adults in addition to the two of you."

They all mentioned the time we spent talking about life issues together, the respect we had in our home for one another, and the fact that we did so many fun things as a family. They all expressed a desire to "not mess that up."

The number one theme in all of our conversations involved the issue of accountability.

They did not want to destroy the good relationships they had with us or other adults they cared about.

It was true our family time was packed with fun activities, mostly outdoors. When you have four boys, you spend a lot of time outside! Boating, fishing, hunting, hiking, camping, exploring the wilderness, science experiments and sports—these were the hallmarks of Schuermann Family Life.

Our boys were blessed to have four grandparents who were all Christians, active in their churches, and of highest character. The boys loved and respected them all. In addition, several men in our church spent time with them.

These men talked to our sons with admiration and respect, treating them as young men rather than little boys. Informally, these adults became accountability groups that our children loved and did not want to lose.

Dr. Kara Powell, Executive Director of Fuller Youth Institute, is considered an expert on the youth culture. She has conducted longitudinal studies on teens that she calls *Sticky Faith* research, looking for a "silver bullet" when it comes to long term faith.[1]

Her studies have focused on the importance of positive intergenerational interactions in the church and in our families. These intergenerational interactions begin with Mom and Dad but should include additional mentor adults.

Dr. Powell's suggestion is Five to One—five trustworthy Christian mentor adults for one teenager. Consider your own children. Who are the adults in their lives? Do they have trustworthy adults who spend time with them one-on-one?

This can be as simple as washing a car together or running an errand. You want wise adults who show an interest in your child as a person and are willing to give them the gift of time.

How can we help adults and young people rub shoulders and share life together? We know the end result is positive. Certainly, in our own household, this was a significant key to managing the teen years and fostering a lasting faith that carried our children into adulthood.

"We will never ascend to an excellent life if we're constantly hanging out with get-by people who are thinking in a mediocre way. We can't be excellent if we follow the world's ways. Excellent people—spiritually minded people who want to excel in their walk with God—hang around excellent people. They spend time with others sharing that same goal"[2] (Tony Evans).

Consider and Apply:

1. It is one thing to be an example, it is quite another thing to have someone desire to follow us. Being an example is of no use if you have no followers. What creates in your children (and others) a desire to follow you?
2. Read II Timothy 3:14, I Corinthians 11:1, and Hebrews 13:7. Remind your children whom they follow will determine their destination. Help them evaluate who is at the front of their parade.

Chapter 36

Be the One Your Children Want to Imitate

When you look a few years down the road, where do you see your children spiritually? Ten, fifteen, even twenty years from now? In Chapter 7, "From Generation to Generation," we noted a message we sometimes hear in our culture today.

The message is *parents have little effect on shaping their children's moral and religious convictions. No matter what parents do, children will make up their own minds.*

Parents may even decide to be religiously neutral to enable their children to make their own decisions. Perhaps these parents believe they have no right to influence. Maybe they hope their children will build stronger convictions if they are allowed to discover and develop them on their own.

Here is the real story: children *will* be shaped. And in the absence of direction from parents, *someone* will shape their thinking. Your influence matters more than you think.

Your children will imitate you, whether or not you are imitating Christ. As parents it is easy for us to think we are falling short in teaching the great truths of Scripture. The foundation for giving this guidance begins when our children are young.

We want them to grow up with solid ground under their feet. Think about how Jesus taught his disciples. He often taught great truths to them simply by explaining what they encountered in their lives.

Mom and Dad, let your children know your thoughts. One powerful way we can do this is to narrate life as we live it before and with our children. Think of the value of having parents talk about the events in their own lives. We need to take time to explain what we do and *why* we do it.

Parents are always teaching because children are always listening and observing. How do you respond to the events, blessings, and annoyances in your life? How do you respond to store clerks, your boss, the government, the not-so-experienced referee in your child's soccer game? Do you show a sincere fondness and love for the people you encounter? You will be a commentary on life. And you will show your children how the puzzle pieces of this life fit together.

Several years ago, we studied the findings of the comprehensive *National Study of Youth and Religion*. This research project was directed by Christian Smith, Professor of Sociology at the University of Notre Dame and Lisa Pearce, Assistant Professor of Sociology at the University of North Carolina at Chapel Hill.

The longitudinal study began in August 2001 and was funded through December 2015. The purpose was to research the shape and influence of religion and spirituality in the lives of American youth and to foster a national discussion about the influence of religion in youth's lives.

In *Handing Down the Faith: How Parents Pass Their Religion on to the Next Generation,* Christian Smith and Amy Adamczyk detail the findings of this study and others.[1]

In a May 2021 article, Smith said, "Among all possible influences, parents exert far and away the greatest influence on their children's religious outcomes...In almost every case, no other institution or program comes close to shaping youth religiously as their parents do—not religious congregations, youth groups, faith-based schools, missions, service trips, summer camps, Sunday School, youth ministers, or anything else."[2] We all know these people and experiences can reinforce a parent's influence, but Smith's research showed they rarely surpass or override it.

Smith said parents matter tremendously, but not just in what we tell our children. Although telling is important, our children are more affected by who we are, by what matters most to us, and the things that are real to us.[3]

It is a combination of who we are, how we live, and what we talk about all together. This tells us that the effect of these valuable ministries to our children will have a greater impact when paired with values they observe in the home.

Indeed... *parents matter.*

The research concluded that just 1% of teens raised by parents who attached little importance to religion were highly religious in their mid-to-late 20s. In contrast, another group of parents talked about faith at home, attached great importance to their beliefs, and were active in their congregations.

Eighty-two percent of children raised by these parents were religiously active as young adults. Christian Smith called this connection "nearly deterministic."[4] The key to raising children who will remain religiously active into their adulthood has been at home all along with parents who take their spiritual responsibility to their children seriously.

If children are a gift from the Lord, the responsibility lies with the parents to provide a God-centered environment in the home. The culture in the home should give the children purpose and propel them to genuine faith in Jesus Christ.

Consider and Apply:

1. Consider the many topics covered in this book. In what ways have you grown spiritually?
2. How are you creating a culture in your home that honors God and will influence future generations?
3. Paul instructed his spiritual children to imitate him. Are you the person you want your children to imitate? How do you become this person?

Conclusion

Finding Ourselves in His Story

"The Bible is one story that unfolds in one book, by one author, about one subject. A story that moves from promise to fulfillment" *(Alistair Begg).*

Any good fiction writer studies the craft of writing including the story arc, character development, beginning-middle-end, conflict and conflict resolution. Though we know God's eternal plan for the world and mankind is not fiction, we see it as a true, cohesive, complete, and beautiful story of redemption.

Each person is eternal, and each person has a story. When God's Spirit is within them and they believe in Jesus Christ, they are gathered up into the greatest story of all. Believing and understanding this narrative will shape every aspect of their lives.

Let's engage the wonderful privilege of instructing our children and not grow weary. We have this privilege for a lifetime. Through this exploration of I Thessalonians 2:1-14, we pray you have clearly seen God's plan for preserving his people by passing on the faith to the next generation and beyond.

Joshua 11:15 says, "Just as the Lord had commanded Moses his servant, so Moses commanded Joshua, and so Joshua did. He left nothing undone of all that the Lord had commanded Moses."

For parents, grandparents, and others who have been entrusted with children, we find our assignment and instruction in the Bible. Wouldn't it be wonderful if we were so commended, and it could be said of us that we left nothing undone of all the Lord commanded us to do?

J.C. Ryle (1816-1900) was a prominent writer, preacher, and Anglican clergyman in nineteenth century Britain. We will close with one of his prayers for parents.

The Lord teach you all how precious Christ is, and what a mighty and complete work He has done for our salvation. Then, I feel confident you will use every means to bring your children to Jesus, that they may live through Him.

The Lord teach you all your need of the Holy Spirit, to renew, sanctify, and quicken your souls. I feel sure you will urge your children to pray for Him without ceasing, and never rest until He has come down into their hearts with power and made them new creatures.

The Lord grant this and then I have good hope that you will indeed train up your children well—train well for this life, and train well for the life to come; train well for earth, and train well for heaven; train them for God, for Christ, and for eternity.[2]

Endnotes

Introduction

1. Charles Spurgeon, *Morning and Evening* (Wheaton, Illinois: Crossway Books, 2003), September 17 Morning.

Chapter 1   Everyone is a Theologian

1. R.C. Sproul, *Everyone's a Theologian: An Introduction to Systematic Theology* (York, Pennsylvania: Reformation Trust Publishing, 2014)
2. A.W. Tozer, *The Knowledge of the Holy* (HarperOne; 31935th edition, 2009) 1.
3. John Stonestreet and Brett Kunkle, *A Practical Guide to Culture: Helping the Next Generation Navigate Today's World* (David C. Cook, 2017) 90.

Chapter 2   From Calling to Boldness

1. John Calvin, Christian Classics Ethereal Library, Calvin's Commentaries on 1 Thessalonians 2:2, Calvin Translation Society edition, Grand Rapids, Michigan https://ccel.org/ccel/calvin/calcom42/calco m42.vi.iv.i.html

2. John Calvin, Christian Classics Ethereal Library, Calvin's Commentaries on Acts of the Apostles, Volume Second, Calvin Translation Society edition, Grand Rapids, Michigan

   https://ccel.org/ccel/calvin/calcom37/calcom37.vi.ii.html

Chapter 3   The Gospel

1. John Piper, "God is Most glorified in Us When We Are Most Satisfied in Him." desiringgod.org, 10/13/2012, https://www.desiringgod.org/messages/god-is-most-glorified-in-us-when-we-are-most-satisfied-in-him.

Chapter 4   Caught in the Devil's Bargain

1. Joni Mitchell. "Woodstock," https://jonimitchell.com/music/song.cfm?id=75

2. John Calvin, Christian Classics Ethereal Library, Calvin's Commentaries on Genesis 1:26, Calvin Translation Society edition, Grand Rapids, Michigan https://ccel.org/ccel/calvin/calcom01/calcom01.vii.i.html

Chapter 5   Raising Little Pharaoh

1. Tom Petty, "It's Good to be King," https://www.tompetty.com/audio/its-good-be-king-682546

2. John Stott, cited from Alistair Begg, "Fathers," truthforlife.org, 1/29/2006, https://www.truthforlife.org/resources/serm on/fathers/

Chapter 6   Our Mission Remains the Same

1. J.R.R. Tolkein *Lord of the Rings: The Fellowship of the Ring Book One* (New York: Houghton Mifflin Company, 1987) 50.

Chapter 7   From Generation to Generation

1. John Piper, "One Generation Shall Praise Your Works to Another." desiringgod.org, March 19, 2000. https://www.desiringgod.org/messages/one-generation-shall-praise-your-works-to-another

2. Alistair Begg, from "The Power of Proper Thinking" podcast, Part 2 of 2, truthforlife.org (also noted on Truth for Life FB and Instagram)

Chapter 8　Congratulations! The Job is Yours!

1. P.D. Eastman, *Flap Your Wings* (Random House Books for Young Readers, 2000)
2. Douglas Wilson, *Standing on the Promises* (Moscow, Idaho: Canon Press, 1997) 9-10.

Chapter 9　Investing the Good News

Chapter 10　Words Matter

1. Paul David Tripp, "Parenting With Mercy" 1/23/2017 https://www.familylife.com/podcast/familyli fe-today/parenting-with-mercy/

Chapter 11　The Power of Validation

1. Rachel Janovic, *Loving the Little Years: Motherhood in the Trenches* (Moscow, Idaho: Canon Press, 2010) 30.
2. Karyn D. Hall and Melissa H. Cook, *The Power of Validation* (New Harbinger Publications, 2012) 12-13.

Chapter 12 Hope Protects and Makes the Heart Glad

1. K. Gallagher, "What is Biblical Hope?"
   https://graceintorah.net/2013/10/26/tikvah-hope/
2. R.C. Sproul, "Our Christian Hope"
   https://www.ligonier.org/learn/devotionals/our-christian-hope/
3. C.S. Lewis, *Mere Christianity* (Harper One, 1952) 134.

Chapter 13 The Gift of Mothers

1. Rebekah Merkle, *Eve in Exile and the Restoration of Femininity* (Moscow, Idaho: Canon Press, 2016) 98.
2. Merkle, *Eve in Exile and the Restoration of Femininity*, 25.
3. John Calvin, Christian Classics Ethereal Library, Calvin's Commentaries on 1 Thessalonians 2:7, Calvin Translation Society edition, Grand Rapids, Michigan https://ccel.org/ccel/calvin/calcom42/calcom42.vi.iv.ii.html

Chapter 14 Mothers and Daughters

1. Rockwell, Norman. *Girl at the Mirror,* 1954. http://www.nrm.org/MT/text/GirlMirror.html
2. Meg Meeker, M.D., *Raising a Strong Daughter in a Toxic Culture:11 Steps to Keep Her Happy, Healthy, and Safe* (Regnery Publishing, 2020) 43.
3. Meeker, *Raising a Strong Daughter in a Toxic Culture:11 Steps to Keep Her Happy, Healthy, and Safe*, 40.

Chapter 15 Mothers and Sons

1. Emerson Eggerichs, *Mother and Son: The Respect Effect* (W Publishing Group, 2016) 14.
2. Eggerichs, *Mother and Son: The Respect Effect*, 15.
3. Eggerichs, *Mother and Son: The Respect Effect*, 16.
4. Douglas Wilson, *Future Men: Raising Boys to Fight Giants* (Moscow, Idaho: Canon Press, 2016) 11.

Chapter 16 Creating Culture

1. Douglas Wilson, *Standing on the Promises* (Moscow, Idaho: Canon Press, 1997) 11.

2. John Stonestreet and Brett Kunkle, *A Practical Guide to Culture: Helping the Next Generation Navigate Today's World* (David C. Cook, 2017) 72.

3. Stonestreet and Kunkle, *A Practical Guide to Culture: Helping the Next Generation Navigate Today's World*, 28.

4. Charles Spurgeon, Morning and Evening (Wheaton, Illinois: Crossway Books, 2003) November 1 Morning.

Chapter 17 A Family That Works

Chapter 18 When Sin Looks Abnormal

1. Tim Challies, "Counterfeit Detection." www.challies.com https://www.challies.com/articles/counterfeit-detection-part-1/ https://www.challies.com/articles/counterfeit-detection-part-2/

2. David F. Wells, *Losing our Virtue* (Wm. B. Eerdmans Publishing Co., 1999) 4.

3. Tim Challies, "Counterfeit Detection, Part 2"
   www.challies.com.
   https://www.challies.com/articles/counterfei
   t-detection-part-2/

Chapter 19   The Gift of Fathers

1. Alistair Begg, "Fathers," truthforlife.org,
   1/29/2006,
   https://www.truthforlife.org/resources/serm
   on/fathers/

Chapter 20   Fathers With Their Sons

1. Douglas Wilson, *Future Men: Raising Boys to
   Fight Giants* (Moscow, Idaho: Canon Press,
   2001) 13-17.

Chapter 21   Fathers With Their Daughters

1. Meg Meeker, M.D., Family Life Today,
   3/14/2016,
   https://www.familylife.com/podcast/familyli
   fe-today/strengthening-the-father-bond/
2. Meg Meeker, *Raising a Strong Daughter in a
   Toxic Culture:11 Steps to Keep Her Happy,
   Healthy, and Safe* (Regnery Publishing, 2020)
   57-68.

Chapter 22 Let the Children Come

1. John Calvin, *Institutes of the Christian Religion* (Grand Rapids, Michigan: Wm. B. Eerdmans Publishing Co., 1989) Book IV, Chapter XVI, Page 533.

Chapter 23 Receiving and Believing

1. Charles Spurgeon, *Morning and Evening* (Wheaton, Illinois: Crossway Books, 2003) December 16 Morning.
2. A.B. Bruce, *The Training of the Twelve* (Grand Rapids, Michigan: Kregel Publications, 1971) 41.
3. Bruce, *The Training of the Twelve*, 24.
4. John Calvin, Christian Classics Ethereal Library, Calvin's Commentaries on Romans, Calvin Translation Society edition, Grand Rapids, Michigan https://ccel.org/ccel/calvin/calcom38/calcom38.v.vi.html

Chapter 24 Living in God's Kingdom

1. R.C. Sproul, "What is the Kingdom of God?" https://www.ligonier.org/blog/what-is-kingdom-god/

Chapter 25 You've Been Charged!

1. R.C. Sproul, citing Martin Luther, "What Does It Mean to Fear God?" https://www.ligonier.org/blog/what-does-it-mean-fear-god/

Chapter 26 Table Talk

1. Ligonier Ministries, *Tabletalk*. https://www.ligonier.org/tabletalk/

Chapter 27 Realistic Expectations

1. Rachel Janovic, *Loving the Little Years: Motherhood in the Trenches* (Canon Press: Moscow, Idaho, 2010) 22-23.
2. Scott Frothingham. "How Long Does It Take for a New Behavior to Become Automatic?" October 24, 2019, European Journal of Social Psychology, https://www.healthline.com/health/how-long-does-it-take-to-form-a-habit#takeaway

Chapter 28 Why Pray?

1. John Calvin, translated by Henry Beveridge, *Institutes of the Christian Religion* (Grand Rapids, Michigan: Wm. B. Eerdmans Publishing Co, 1989) Book III, Chapter XX, Page 146.

2. Charles Spurgeon, *Morning and Evening* (Wheaton, Illinois: Crossway Books, 2003) Morning Dec 5.

3. Calvin, *Institutes of the Christian Religion*, Book III, Chapter XX, Page 158.

Chapter 29 Gaining Confidence in Prayer

1. John Calvin, translated by Henry Beveridge, *Institutes of the Christian Religion* (Grand Rapids, Michigan: Wm. B. Eerdmans Publishing Co., 1989) Book III, Chapter XX, Page 153.

2. Calvin, *Institutes of the Christian Religion*, Book III, Chapter XX, Page 155.

3. Calvin, *Institutes of the Christian Religion*, Book III, Chapter XX, Page 150.

Chapter 30 Rejoice Over Them

Chapter 31 Nurturing a Desire for Instruction

Chapter 32 How the Word Works

Chapter 33   The Spirit at Work

1. Westminster Confession of Faith, 1646, Chapter II, Of God, and of the Holy Trinity, Section III. https://www.ligonier.org/learn/articles/214e stminster-confession-faith/
2. Sinclair B. Ferguson, *The Holy Spirit: Contours of Christian Theology* (Downers Grove, Illinois: InterVarsity Press, 1996) 71.
3. Charles Spurgeon, *Morning and Evening* (Wheaton, Illinois: Crossway Books, 2003) Morning January 15.
4. John Calvin, translated by Henry Beveridge, *Institutes of the Christian Religion* (Grand Rapids, Michigan: Wm. B. Eerdmans Publishing Co., 1989) Book III, Chapter I, Page 466.

Chapter 34   What Are You Training Them to Hunt?

Chapter 35   Surviving the Teen Years

1. Kara Powell, https://fulleryouthinstitute.org/stickyfaith/
2. Tony Evans, commenting on Philippians 3:15-17. *The Tony Evans Bible Commentary* (Nashville, Tennessee: Holman Bible Publishers, 2019) 1244.

Chapter 36 Be the One Your Children Want to Imitate

1. Christian Smith and Amy Adamczyk, *Handing Down the Faith: How Parents Pass Their Religion on to the Next Generation* (New York: Oxford University Press, 2021)
2. Christian Smith, "Keep the Faith," www.firstthings.com, https://www.firstthings.com/article/2021/05/keeping-the-faith
3. Smith, "Keep the Faith." www.firstthings.com
4. David Briggs, interview with Christian Smith, "Parents are Top Influence in Teens Remaining Active in Religion as Young Adults" www.christiancentury.org, https://www.christiancentury.org/article/2014-11/parents-no-1-influence-teens-remaining-religiously-active-young-adults

Conclusion

1. Alistair Begg, https://www.azquotes.com/quote/894718
2. J.C. Ryle, *The Duties of Parents* (Ichthus Publications, 2014) 48.

Stan and Cheryl Schuermann devoted themselves for over four decades to the teaching ministry at their local church. Since 1999, they have focused on teaching and encouraging parents.

Stan holds an M.S. from Oklahoma State University in Personnel and Guidance. He retired early from a professional career in hospital administration to allow more time for writing and ministry.

Cheryl earned an M.S. from Oklahoma State University in Curriculum and Instruction. A career educator and literacy consultant, she now embraces this season of writing. Cheryl is the author of *When the Water Runs: Growing Up With Alaska* (Pen It! Publications, 2019) and two books for children.

The Schuermanns raised four sons, have four lovely daughters-in-law, and enjoy the blessings of thirteen grandchildren. Their favorite place to write and play is the family country retreat affectionately known as The Farm.